DIRTY
WEEKENDS

DIRTY
WEEKENDS

or The Part-Time Gardener

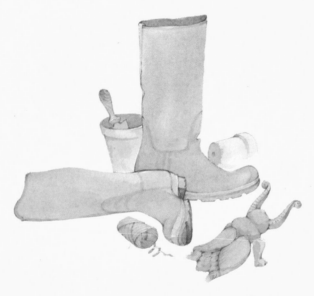

Written and Illustrated by Sarah Creswell

B L O O M S B U R Y

For Simon

I would like to thank the many friends who have so generously
let me potter and paint in their gardens, especially John and Sue Willows,
Kathleen McCall McCowan, Emma and John Poë, Joanna and
Peter Sebag-Montefiore and Albinia Diggle. My thanks go to
Madeleine Miles for typing the book. I have a debt of gratitude to Francis Burne
for so very many reasons. I would also like to express my heartfelt appreciation to
my family for their support: Miranda, Alexander and Sophia who have so
cheerfully put up with domestic chaos; my mother-in-law for her
gardening wisdom and my mother for her unfailing support and
encouragement; Miss Lewis (Loulou), who taught me to paint, and, for
that matter, to write; my uncles, Arthur Collins who gave me so many
good gardening reference books over the years which have been invaluable
to me, and Harry Stanley, who started me off down the primrose path
by giving me my first commission; my dear aunts; and finally my beloved brother,
Peter Stanley, a great supporter and a fellow plantaholic.

First published in Great Britain 1987
Copyright © 1987 by Sarah Creswell

Bloomsbury Publishing Ltd, 2 Soho Square, London W1V 5DE

British Library Cataloguing in Publication Data

Creswell, Sarah
Dirty weekends: or the part-time gardener
1. Gardening
I. Title
635   SB450.97

ISBN 0-7475-0102-5

Two lines of verse on page 21 by W. H. Davies (1870–1940) from *Collected
Poems* © 1963 Jonathan Cape Ltd., reprinted by permission of Jonathan Cape
Ltd. on behalf of Mrs H. M. Davies and Wesleyan University Press.

Designed by Fielding Rowinski
Phototypeset by Butler & Tanner Ltd, Frome and London
Printed and Bound in Italy

Contents

Our England is a garden,
and such gardens are not made
By singing – 'Oh, how beautiful!'
and sitting in the shade,
When better men than we go out
and start their working lives
At grubbing weeds from gravel paths
with broken dinner-knives.

Then seek your job with thankfulness
and work till further orders,
If it's only netting strawberries
or killing slugs on borders;
And when your back stops aching
and your hands begin to harden
You will find yourself a partner
in the Glory of the Garden.

Oh, Adam was a gardener,
and God who makes him sees
That half a proper gardener's work
is done upon his knees;
So when your work is finished,
you can wash your hands and pray
For the Glory of the Garden,
that it may not pass away.

Rudyard Kipling

Introduction

ONE SUNDAY EVENING, driving back to London on the motorway, discussing our somewhat hectic afternoon's gardening and its legacy of aching backs and engrained fingernails, my husband said – after a short silence – 'Why don't you write a book on weekend gardening?' Immediately he overtook a sluggish Morris Minor. I can never concentrate while he is overtaking; I become convinced that we will never arrive safely at our destination, which is mean spirited of me when I think that we have only had two minor accidents during our married life. One involved a carload of nuns, and the other a disabled person. I thought this must be symbolic, but I was still not sure of what.

Several service stations later the idea had sunk into my consciousness, and I began to think how many people were in a position similar to ours, where it is only possible to tend one's plot, garden or allotment at the weekend. Our garden is in Dorset, where we return like snapped knicker elastic each weekend from our working lives in London. Many people work hard during the week with long hours and tiring commuting journeys, and so can only find time to garden during weekends, or part-time during some days or evenings.

There are also those with allotments a little way away from their houses. They are in a happier situation than the weekend commuter, but may only be able to visit their plots once or twice in mid-week. It is with such gardeners in mind that I have written this book.

Enthusiastic weekend gardeners return to their roots late on a Friday night. Having unloaded the car, maybe let out the dog, cat or budgerigar (maybe not), they seize a cup (or glass) of liquid refreshment and rush out into the garden, with or without a torch depending on the season, to see what happiness or disaster has occurred during the week.

I will never forget the joy of having planted a lawn in our newly acquired garden which had been completely neglected since the war. We had poisoned and rotivated all summer and sowed the lawn seed in September after a month of no rain at all. We sent up little prayers to St Francis asking him to direct his birds to someone else's seeded patch, and to whoever the local rain-maker might be. A miracle happened, and the next two days were drizzly and damp, followed by a good hard downpour. This, combined with warm earth, germinated the lawn and one weekend I was woken up by my husband at six o'clock on Saturday morning – we had arrived too late on the Friday to do the torchlight inspection – saying 'It's green.' Dragging myself out of a lovely warm bed, I went to the window – and it was. In fact it was exactly two months from sow to mow, due not to any expertise, but to the luck of

Alstroemeria (Peruvian lily)

the elements (or our prayers?). Not all our projects have turned out so successfully, but, as all weekend gardeners know, part of the excitement and challenge of this way of gardening lies in the gambles that must be taken against rain, greenfly or frost.

So, with modesty, I have tried to deal with the problems, and to offer shortcuts and helpful hints that we have come across during our few years as enthusiastic – but semi-absent – guardians of a small garden three hours away from London.

Of necessity, this book is set within the framework of a weekend or part-time garden. The plants I describe and have painted will mostly grow anywhere and everywhere, given luck and freedom from rabbits, deer and natural hazards. Occasional gardening is a calculated risk and therein lies the joy and excitement, equally well the reward. You will clothe this framework and, according to your preferences, energy, and the help of your good gardening friends, you will nurture the never finished and always changing personality of your garden.

I hope that in writing this book I have not offended friends and relations who cherish in their garden the very things that I have castigated, such as bare rose-beds and garish marigolds. Forgive me; if you love them, they must be beautiful. I may also have caused gardeners more experienced and wiser than myself to shake their heads in horror at the ignorance of a mere amateur. Forgive me, for one learns something new every gardening day, and remember that we are all bound by a common link – the love of cultivation.

Planning

LTHOUGH IT IS rare that anyone exactly follows advice on planning a garden to the letter, it is better to have a broad but flexible idea of what you hope to achieve overall, rather than a patchwork. Not only will your mistakes prove expensive, but a lot of precious time goes into moving plants and shrubs planted in the wrong position and you will perhaps lose a year's good growing time by planting something that you like in an inappropriate position where it just survives. Plants and shrubs must flourish for the weekender or occasional gardener – there is no time for an intensive care ward.

Later in this chapter we will dwell on trouble-free plants and shrubs, but to begin with let us think about soil, and aspects and types of garden.

SOIL

You will have a rough idea of the composition of your soil. If you are starting afresh with a newly acquired property, you will be well repaid by walking around the vicinity of your new abode to note what your neighbours are growing. You should then visit the gardens nearby which are open to the public – they also occasionally offer plants for sale, which are often better rooted and more unusual than commercially grown plants from garden centres and nurseries. The third avenue of investigation is to take a walk in the surrounding countryside and look carefully at the indigenous wild flowers. A lot can be learned from them. Wild honeysuckle, roses, old man's beard (wild clematis), willow, bluebells, primroses, poppies and many more, all have their domesticated equivalents. Need you look further for indications as to what will thrive in your particular patch?

Finally, it is well worthwhile using a soil-testing kit to determine the p.H of your garden – that is to say, the degree of acidity or alkalinity of the soil – so as to decide which plants will be happy with you. To put it simply, neutral soil has a p.H of 7.0. Below this figure the soil is acid, and above it the soil is alkaline.

Do test the soil in various places, for even in quite a small area the soil can change, and this can affect where you decide to plant your newly acquired treasure. The Royal Horticultural Society at Wisley, Surrey, will test your soil for you for a small charge, and this can be quite interesting.

A sandy soil will dry out quickly and will need plenty of humus and manure to provide nourishment. A clay soil will probably be rich in nutrients, but when wet will remain waterlogged, and when dry will crack. Therefore clay soils will need the addition of compost humus and sharp sand to break it up, and to prevent it becoming like cement during a hot, dry summer. You can buy a geological map of your area,

Papaver somniferum (opium poppy)

but this will satisfy your curiosity only on a large scale. You will probably need a more detailed assessment.

It is easy to ascertain with a brief glance whether you can grow rhododendrons, azaleas, and camellias and heathers, the calcifuges, or whether chalk and lime-loving plants must be your forte. The effort of studying the composition of your soil a little more closely is well worthwhile, without too much wallowing in scientific knowledge.

ASPECT

Now that you have discovered the type or types of soil that you have to work with, consider the aspect of your garden. Does it face north,

Azalea mollis

south, east or west? Where does the prevailing wind come from? Natural dampness of the plot, sloping ground, and sun and shade must also come into your calculations. Bear in mind that newly planted trees, shrubs and plants may suffer or die, because you will not be able to water them sufficiently during the period that they need to get their roots down. This is not an insuperable problem but one which is worth taking into account if you wish your plants to thrive. If you are blessed with walls, rejoice, for your opportunities for gardening both horizontally and vertically are doubled, and you may gain some protection from icy winds. Of course you may end up with a frost pocket, but there is a maggot in nearly every raspberry.

Slugs and snails are a sore trial if you have walls, for they seem to love this kind of habitat and can really make a banquet on your bulbs and hostas. There are, however, ways and means of dealing with this problem, depending on your taste. Ashes deter these 'slimeys', as do grit and gravel, for slugs and snails have tender undersides, and dislike a surface that is abrasive. I am afraid I ruthlessly fling down blue slug pellets – the blue colour deters birds so they will not be harmed by them and I have found that dogs sensibly avoid these pellets. Nothing is so unsightly as a chewed up hosta leaf and one could weep when one finds all the tender heads of hyacinths and tulips nibbled away just as they are about to come into flower – so death to the slugs and snails.

If you are fortunate enough to have a stream, be thankful, for, although your weeds and stranglers will run riot, the weekend watering problem will be halved.

If your garden is very exposed, you may well want to think about short-term measures such as chestnut paling, or other fencing; medium-term measures, such as planting hedges and windbreaks; and finally long-term measures, such as planting thick shrubs and trees.

The joy of visiting and enjoying other people's gardens stems from the unique combination of conditions that each individual gardener has had to come to terms with: these problems of light and shade, wind and damp, and soil, which mean that no two gardens are alike. Even in building developments which start out with gardens which are all of a similar size and shape, everyone has a slightly different problem. In addition the owners have different tastes as to climbers, herbaceous plants and so on, usually reflecting the influences of their friends' or relations' gardens, the smells of childhood nostalgia, and so many other factors. I continuously find this as fascinating as the fact that the good God gave us all two eyes, a nose and a mouth, and yet the permutations of our faces are such that no two are alike.

TYPES

If one has to define various types of gardens one must, sadly, generalize in order to simplify. As this book is primarily for weekend gardeners who cannot depend on help, the gardens that we are talking about will probably be fairly small.

It is very frustrating to have to spend precious weekend time mowing the lawn when there are a thousand and one other gardening jobs which are crying out to be done. We are lucky enough to have a neighbour who mows our lawn once a week during the summer and this is a great luxury. If you can afford to pay someone and if you live near or in a village, it is not difficult to find a mower-person, for it is a job which can be done any time during the week, depending on the elements. If you are unable to cut the lawn due to rain or other commitments, you will find yourself becoming paranoid during the following week – waking up in the early hours with visions of fighting your way through a hayfield. The majority of readers are not aiming at achieving a lawn like the centre court of Wimbledon, but they know that grass makes a charming foil to borders and shrubs, rather as a mount or frame enhances a painting.

Do not think of a garden as being a horizontal creation – the vertical aspect lends interest, the flat garden is boring. Trees, shrubs, walls and climbing plants will transform the most ordinary plot, and during the winter months will provide an elegant skeleton, giving you inspiration, and hope, for the excitement of spring. Your challenge will begin with the shape of your garden. Do not despair if, for example, your plot is oblong and flat; one of the most interesting gardens that I have painted was just such a shape, and its owner had placed a large mirror on the end wall with a paved path leading around to it, and plants grown in and alongside the paving. With climbers obliterating the edges of the mirror, the effect from the house was a *trompe l'oeil* giving infinite length as the path and plants were reflected in the mirror. Theatrical? Not a whit, to my mind. It is a cunning solution, aesthetically pleasing, and far better than a claustrophobic blank wall.

If your garden is badly drained, you have the opportunity to make a bog-garden and emphasize and capitalize on this, making a fault into an asset.

Your garden dries up too much? There are so many plants, from the sedum to more exotic fellows, who will thrive in this sort of situation.

And if your garden is on pure chalk or acid soil, enlarge on this, it is an advantage: do not try to fight it but make the most of what you have got. A little common sense, combined with imagination, will transform your ideas, seeded in wakeful hours or in the bath, into a reality which will give joy, not only to yourself but to your visitors.

Every weekend gardener has to find their own solution to the problems of the distance that they live from their garden, and the time they will be able, at a guess, to expend on it. Remembering that herbaceous borders, grassy paths and rose gardens are the most labour-intensive form of gardening, this does not rule out a combination of these elements if you are sufficiently enthusiastic about them. It merely means that you will have less time for other work. If, for example, you are often away travelling, you may have to find a labour-saving solution to prevent you returning to a Paradise Lost kind of garden, resembling an ecological jungle of convolvulus, nettles and brambles. I hope that you will find ideas to help you in these pages.

Many weekend gardens are composed largely of a paved area with tubs and these can look spectacular as well as having the advantage of being movable. Of course, it depends on the size of your tubs, but this kind of gardening is low in maintenance and can be very effective.

We cannot grow camellias owing to the chalk in our soil, but they grow happily in a beer barrel sawn in half filled with peat compost, and I have undersown C. 'Donation' with Meconopsis baileyi, the lovely sky-blue poppy (another peat-lover), enabling us to enjoy two calcifuges without cosseting. Another good tub planting, apart from the obvious solution of pelargoniums and petunias, and so on, are miniature roses. I love these little souls; they are seen to advantage in a tub, and flower and re-flower prolifically. But they must be adequately fertilized if they are to repeat flower.

The great Mrs Gertrude Jekyll, who transformed the ideas of Victorian formal gardening with its wealth of bedding-out plants in formal designs to more natural and permanent planting, had many good ideas which we can copy, on a more modest scale. She had a part of the garden reserved, out of sight, for those plants which she was bringing on, or those whose flowering season was over. When there was a gap in the herbaceous or mixed border, she had no qualms about filling this in with plants from her 'reserve' beds, often in pots plunged into the earth, easy to lift and transplant to avoid the situation every gardener knows – a patchy bed of 'has-beens' or hopefuls. How often do we all echo the immortal words of Ruth Draper who told her guests that they should have seen the garden a fortnight ago, when it was a picture. Admittedly, Gertrude Jekyll had armies of gardeners but we may well take a leaf out of her book by making an unobtrusive reserve bed in some hidden corner, if we have a metre or two of space full of goodies

to pop into the border to rejuvenate it; also, let's face it, to impress some weekend visitor. Instant gardening is not to be sneezed at for the weekender. If the reserve plot appeals to you, keep your lily and other summer bulbs there in their pots – in this way you will not lose them or dig them up in a fit of absentmindedness when their leaves have died down. You can then bring pots of good scented lilies onto your terrace, or into your house, when the time is ripe, as well as into your border. I invest in some good lily bulbs each autumn, plant them in enriched compost, sink them into my plunge bed and cover the pots with a layer

Lonicera americana (honeysuckle)

of ashes. You can then forget about them until they come into bud, when you lift the pots and revel in the beauty and the fragrance for a few weeks. You can finally banish the dreary 'has-beens' back to their plunge bed to sleep happily until the following year. This ploy looks impressive, but is perfectly simple.

You may also use this little plot for taking cuttings, in which case a trench of mixed peat and sharp sand will provide the ideal rooting soil. The whole subject of propagation is fascinating but probably best dealt with elsewhere, as our weekend gardeners are busy people, with many claims on their time.

If you find that your garden is getting too much for you and that you are rapidly spiralling downwards into a nervous breakdown – think again, and re-assess your priorities. The answer is 'shrink': shrink away from the garden into the house for a start. Pour yourself a strong drink and think about the future. Shrink into low-maintenance shrubs for all-round colour of foliage and flowers, underplanted with bulbs, instead of your always-wanting-to-be-weeded border. Shrink into a rockery where the weeds can be kept at bay with gravel and stones and spot weedkiller wands. Shrink into paving stones with splashes of colour in the cracks from self-seeding plants, such as Alyssum, dwarf variegated grasses, Alchemilla, Feverfue, forget me nots, Aquilegias, and so on, so that you can admire the results from your deckchair and recite:

> What is this life, if full of care,
> We have no time to stand and stare?

As I write, I have a vision of a Greek chorus of garden gnomes rising up from the rockery and replying:

> A garden is a lovely thing
> and gardens are not made
> By singing 'Oh how beautiful'
> and sitting in the shade.

Away with fantasy, back to reality, and the Great Shrink. Shrink to pots, tubs, sinks and self-watering containers (perhaps augmented from your reserve bed?). You will be amazed at what will grow well in a tub or barrel. Fig trees in a sunny position are very happy as their roots need to be restricted. Camellias, planted in a peat compost, are beautiful during the flowering season and their leaves are attractive during the rest of the year as a foil for underplanting with a variety of plants.

Hostas are good plants to grow in pots if well fertilized, and of course lilies are ideal. Do combine a mass of potted plants in a good group –

varying size, colour and shape to make an impact which can be changed throughout the seasons.

While you are in your shrinking-thinking frame of mind, imagine sculptural artichokes: beautiful and grey-leaved (and good to eat), riotous runner beans with their vivid scarlet flowers, and beet for garnet-red foliage and stalks, as an unusual tub planting.

Imagine height in your barrels or tubs too. With three canes tied as a pyramid, you can train morning glories, nasturtiums, Cobea scandens or passion flower (Passiflora caerulea) into pyramids of colour during high summer, or, for longer lasting plantings, honeysuckle, jasmine or climbing roses. Another simple but effective construction which you may care to erect in a decent-sized tub is an umbrella-like frame nailed atop a post. Climbing plants growing up this can make a stunning display, either with perennials or with plants such as ivy-leaved geraniums or tender passion flowers; and of course they have to be brought inside during the winter. If this is not possible then the answer is to use hardy climbers.

So, 'shrink' is the operative word – each in his own way, depending on circumstances. Your garden should be a place to enjoy, to recharge your batteries, a place of pleasure and peace, and hope for the next weekend, for the next season, for the next year. It must not become a chore or a millstone around your neck: organize your garden so that you can love it and live with it.

Borders

F OR THE WEEKEND gardener the ideal mature border is one where after a year or two of back-breaking weeding, the plants knit up to provide clumps and ground cover and virtually no bare earth is left, stifling the weed seedlings.

Alchemilla mollis is a 'clumper' which no garden should be without. It is easy to grow, not too invasive, and its lime-green foliage provides a marvellous background for almost every neighbouring plant. There is no prettier sight than dew or rain drops on the leaves of the Alchemilla: they stay like diamonds long after the sun has dried the leaves of others. Alchemilla is so called because the alchemists of yore believed that the dew on the leaves was very pure. Coming from condensation, it is as pure as you can find in nature, more so than rainwater which becomes acid as it falls. I can understand the belief, and appreciate the origin of the name. Another plant – really belonging to the herb garden – which has this fairy-like quality is fennel. I love to see this feather-leaved herb sparkling with drops of rain. One is, after all, creating a garden for beauty, and beauty can be found in unexpected places. Sempervivums hold their rain or dew drops in a delightful way as well. This may be some consolation when the garden as a whole looks damp and soggy.

Another 'clumper' which will fill out a circle of at least two feet in diameter within two years is the family of cranesbill. In other words, the hardy geraniums. These are delightful characters, dying away during the winter, but returning better than ever every spring. When you feel that they are well-established you will gain lasting friendships from dividing them and giving away clumps to your acquaintances. The cranesbill geraniums flower in early summer, although a scattering of flowers will re-appear later, and the foliage remains. They will grow in any well-drained soil in an open sunny position, and many will grow in shadier places. They provide a really beautiful show of flowers lasting about a month or two with a spectrum of colour ranging from pure white through the lavenders, purples and pinks to deep blue.

There is such a wealth of choice amongst hardy geraniums that it is really worth while consulting a specialist nursery catalogue (one such is the Sandwich Nursery in Kent), so that you may choose according to your colour scheme and preference as to height and position. Geranium pratense 'Plenum Album' grows to a height of about two feet, as does the beautiful blue one, G. ibericum, which flowers conveniently in late summer. There are several white ones which will enliven a shady border. There is the well known 'Johnson's Blue' with vivid flowers, there are trailing plants, there are ones with especially attractive foliage, and so the list goes on. All are trouble-free and a boon for the low-maintenance gardener.

Geranium pratense 'Johnson's blue' (hardy geranium)

It must be remembered when planting both Alchemilla and hardy geraniums that they will smother and over-lay anything planted near them when they come into 'full clump', having seemed invisible during the winter. G. maderense, which is evergreen, is the exception. It is hard to imagine in the so-called dead season that such a spectacular burst of growth will transform a dormant plant into a cushion of colour. A good hint for the more absent-minded gardener is to plant a bamboo stake in the epicentre of these clumps before the leaves die away in the autumn, and then keep your new plants well away from this, otherwise your precious treasures will be overwhelmed.

I would make a plea for the planting of grey or lime-green plants in the border to tone down and compensate strong colours. I remember being told at art school that Rubens said he could paint the most delicate flesh tones with mud colours, as long as he could choose the adjacent pigments. The same principle applies to the planning of a border.

GREY PLANTS

The rue, Ruta graveolens 'Jackman's Blue', has a soft blue-grey foliage and is a good foil all summer. It grows best in a sunny position and will reach two feet high or more if pruned in April. Rue is often evergreen and fairly hardy. There is a variegated version, R. graveolens 'Variegata' – both are good for picking during the winter, and make a beautiful foil for all herbaceous plants. Rue is really a small shrub and can be pruned to a good round or small standard shape.

The bluey-green Hosta seiboldiana 'Elegans' is a good sculptural plant covering a large circumference, if you can keep slugs and snails from the leaves on which they love to feast. The bonus of this good foliage plant is the pale, soft mauve spikes of flowers in July. The Hosta dies down completely in winter, so do remember not to plant too close to it, for anything underneath its large leaves will never see the light of day.

The Hosta family, although greedy for food and susceptible to slugs, are trouble-free plants and hardy, suitable for sunny or shady positions. You may like H. fortunei which also has blue-grey leaves; H. lancifolia Variegata which has dark green leaves edged with white; or H. undulata with twisted variegated leaves. H. Plantiginea has white fragrant flowers, and you will find other members of this 'Corfu Lily' family. Personally, I love H. seiboldiana 'Elegans', but find the tortured H. undulata slightly disturbing.

The 'cotton lavender' is cursed with an appalling Latin name, as difficult to pronouce as it is to spell – Santolina chamaecyparissus to be exact. (One feels that it ought to be a village in Wales.) However, the plant itself is an undemanding evergreen or, rather, evergrey. Like most silver or grey-leaved plants, it thrives best in full sun, and the purists sometimes cut off the flowers. I personally like the small yellow pom-pom heads which appear if you omit to prune it. The foliage is delightful in itself and is aromatic to boot. It is essential to prune back hard in the late spring some years so that your santolina does not become straggly. There are several other varieties, most with good grey feathery foliage and also aromatic. Tanacetum, of the chrysanthemum family, is another good grey, hardy herbaceous plant.

Artemisia, an aromatic grey-green filigree-leaved shrub, makes a wonderful foil for the flowers in your border, happily quashing the weeds underneath. A. 'Lambrook Silver' I like best for its colouring, but if you have a place by a path where you can pinch the leaves as you walk, plant A. absinthium which has such a delicious smell. A. arborescens 'Powis Castle' is another favourite. The Artemisias are commonly known as wormwood, or tarragon, and are easy to grow if planted in a sunny position, regardless of soil. The only thing they dislike is damp shade. Tarragon, the herb, used in cooking and in flavouring vinegar, goes by the slightly scary name of Artemisia dracunculus, and sprigs can be dried or deep frozen. The attractive foliage of many herbs can aid you if you have a sunny spot near your kitchen door to plant herbs either in a bed or in pots. Bearing in mind that many herbs have Mediterranean or southern origins and are therefore sun-lovers, albeit hardy, you may care to introduce them into your beds or terrace. Variegated mint, golden thyme, rosemary, chives and rue

Alchemilla mollis, Chrysanthemum parthenium aureum (golden feverfue), *Cineraria maritima*

are but a few of the delightful and useful plants which spring to mind. Be wary of the bay tree, which can grow quite large if planted in good soil. If you have visions of charming standard or pyramidical bays in pots, take a look at the upwardly mobile, fresh-faced, muesli-eating districts of any large city, and count the number of expensive little bay trees in pots with browned-off leaves slowly dying through lack of water or food, or as a result of frost-withered roots which can't find sanctuary far enough underground.

Helichrysum is another small shrub with soft grey foliage, often aromatic. Again, this shrub likes the sun and doesn't mind the poorest of soils. H. plicatum has the best foliage if we are searching for a silver-grey background. H. augustifolium has a less pleasing foliage, more sage-green, but the smell which has earned it the name of the 'curry plant' is, to me, a special attraction.

I would not be without a few bushes of lavender in my garden; all Lavandula will grow in any well drained, preferably sunny spot and their soft grey foliage is gentle on the eye the whole year around, being semi-evergreen. The superb bonus of this charming shrub comes during its flowering season in late July/August. The evocative scent of lavender will give you great joy, so it seems wrong not to give garden room to this trouble-free and easy-going shrub. I prune my lavenders back as soon as the flowers begin to fade, keeping the heads in a bowl to scent the house. One should be quite severe in pruning, for a compact cushion of lavender is so much more attractive than a straggly bush.

If you can plant these aromatic shrubs next to steps, a path or terrace where you are likely to touch or feel them as you pass, your enjoyment of them will be doubled. In the same context, I love rosemary planted somewhere 'touchable', and sweet-smelling geraniums in a hallway.

Anaphalis is a hardy perennial which will spread itself. Its leaves are silvery-green and woolly and it bears clusters of tiny white flowers in August. Anaphalis comes into flower at a timely moment when there could well be a gap in your border. However, if you can bear to, pick the stalks in full flower, and strip off the leaves, tie some raffia around them and hang them up to dry, with the heads hanging downwards. These flowers dry with ease and are invaluable for vases during the winter months, or in a dark corner or bathroom. They keep their fresh whiteness, even when dried, for at least a year. I like A. nubigena for preference, as it is shorter and less leggy than other varieties.

Senecio cineraria maritima has a pearly white foliage and is a beautiful foil in borders, tubs or window boxes but is best grown as an annual and planted each spring, not being tremendously hardy. I buy a box full of these every spring from the new Covent Garden at Nine Elms. If your mind is dwelling on grey foliage, do not forget the pinks, which are dealt with in detail on page 42.

Stachys lanata, commonly known as lambs' ears, is a good grey standby well known by all – I love it but I wish its furry grey leaves didn't look so disconsolate and bedraggled after rain. However, it has an attractive texture and colour in dry weather and is an easy plant to grow in a sunny spot on any well drained soil.

LIME-GREEN PLANTS

Apart from Alchemilla mollis, which is a great favourite of mine, although so common now, there are other beautiful yellowy green plants whose foliage makes an ideal foil throughout the summer. One of the more charming is the lime-green version of the feverfue; the ordinary green-leaved plant is dull, but the vivid Chrysanthemum parthenium aureum looks splendid against stone and if you obtain one good plant you will have the bonus of dozens of self-sown plantlets the following year. Although feverfue will sow itself endlessly in all sorts of unlikely places, it is not an invasive plant, for you may easily dig it up when unwanted. The foliage is brilliant during the months of May and June after which it will produce myriads of little daisy-like flowers,

Dianthus 'Doris' (modern pink)

so refreshing on the eye during hot days. When the flowers have died, you cut them off, an easy job, and new fresh lime-green leaves will grace your garden until the first frosts. In fact, this year I have had plantlets of feverfue nestling in paths and walls looking cheerful in February, and lightening the grey and gloomy overall view of the garden. An accommodating plant, infallible in any garden with some sun, and the leaves are a cure for migraine, so I am assured.

Another lime-green, or really more golden plant, is the form of creeping jenny called Lysimachia nummularia Aurea. This grows thickly and very low on the ground and is useful as a cover crop. It greens up early in the spring and bears a vivid golden flower along all its creeping branches in June and July. It is vigorous and will cover a large area within a year or two but is easy to eliminate where unwanted. I love this little creeping jenny which gives the impression of sunshine on the greyest day.

A favourite plant of mine, both for its foliage and its flowers, is the Euphorbia. One of the most magnificent plants in the border is Euphorbia wulfenii – you will need to have enough room to accommodate this for after three years he will have grown to about three feet by four feet and will be set to make a take-over bid. However, one can always restrain him by pruning and taking cuttings by layering, for example

Nigella damascena
(love in the mist)

by pinning down a branch to the earth until it roots. Euphorbia wolfenii has soft blue-green leaves, and spectacular lime-green flowers in the shape of a mop of florets, each head about six inches in circumference. These appear in late May or early June and retain their proud beauty for two months. This plant has a magnificent and sculptural presence which is very individual and impressive. There are numerous other varieties of Euphorbia of all sizes and shapes – a very spectacular one is E. characias with blue-grey foliage and lime-green flowers in May and June, making a three feet by four feet plant. E. polychroma is smaller and brings forth florets of an almost fluorescent lime-green. Like an iced lolly, it makes you feel quite refreshed even to look at it on a hot and humid day.

Finally, an indispensable border shrub: the hardy fuchsia. Hardy fuchsia disappear completely during the winter and one always fears that they are dead, but have patience, they re-appear with renewed vigour every summer and accommodatingly delight you with a pro-fusion of blooms throughout August and September in border or pot. My favourite fuchsia are F. magellicana with its long slender flowers (there is a variegated form as well), and F. magellicana Versicolor which has soft grey-green leaves tinged with pink. These hardy fuchsias grow in the most elegant fashion, their arching branches dripping with flowers. Ideal for the part-timer, for they are remarkably undemanding.

Borders are ever-changing spectrums like the magical kaleidoscopes a child holds to its eye to marvel at the jewelled pattern; shake the toy and the pattern changes, shake again and the permutations are endless. Plants grow, plants die, you add and subtract, you prune, and you will find that this year your borders will be quite different from the ones that you worried or enthused over the year before. Next year the picture will change again; the colours that you thought were so compatible may clash because the spring has come late, and the vivid puce hardy geraniums will have lingered to compete with the tawny Hemerocallis. So you plan to re-arrange in the autumn, in case the same weather pattern continues, and you carry on doing your juggling act season after season. Such is the challenge and the fascination for the plantaholic.

Just occasionally, with a combination of good luck and inspiration, you will achieve an effect which satisfies you. At that moment it is a good idea to jot down on a piece of paper or in a gardening diary, just what has pleased you, and to try and capitalize on the effect the next year. The never-ending search for perfection is what makes an enthusiastic gardener so hopeful. One can almost imagine the cartoon balloon emerging from the gardener's head, proclaiming, 'Next year I can do better.'

I pass on a combination of planting in our south-facing border in September, which has struck me as worthwhile pursuing. Imagine Galtonia candicans rising majestically above white and blue Agapanthus with Gypsophila 'Bristol Fairy', which for the first time has consented to flower for me, and in front the tiny creeping white rose, 'Snow Carpet'. Combined with silver Artemisia, Nepeta and Anaphalis, lime-green Euphorbia polychroma and feverfue, with small bushes of lavender intermingled with self-sown love in the mist, this made a gentle coloured haze of flowers, easy on the eye, and beloved by the bees during the good days of September. It may not happen like this next year, the slugs may eat the Galtonias, but I will file the effect away in my memory, and shall hope to improve upon it.

Annuals and Perennials

E LOVE THE ANNUALS in the summer months, although not planted like a municipal garden. One mustn't decry municipal gardening; some of it is extremely imaginative, but a lot is geometrically planted with hideous shades of orange marigolds, zinnias and puce petunias interspersed with lobelia. All of these plants are attractive if planted with cool green nicotianas or soft greys (with perhaps the exception of orange marigolds) but so often the effect is garish, and in straight lines and dots. The loveliest planting of roundabouts that I have seen was in New Delhi in February, where the profusion of annuals was breathtaking – there were all the usual ones that one knows so well from this country, no doubt the legacy of the memsahibs to their malis, but planted with such gusto that one could only imagine that kilos of seed had just been scattered on the warm ground after the monsoons.

We cheat as regards the annuals, and I have no shame in admitting that I buy boxfuls early in the season from the new Covent Garden. There is no way that you can tend seeds if you are away from your seed trays from Monday to Friday, so one must be realistic in order to achieve one's object – a lovely garden. If you are not within reach of Nine Elms there will be other wholesale markets within your orbit, and all good garden centres sell boxes of annuals in the spring. Do buy plentifully and think big, even in the smallest garden. I plant annuals much closer together than the gardening books advise; the purpose of the annual is to provide splashes of colour, not dots, and the closer together you plant, the less room there is for weeds.

Everyone will have their favourite annuals, so I will just tell you about my own, and you will work out your own yearly scheme when you have experimented with the plants that like your garden. The majority of annuals are not choosy as to their soil, but wind, rain and drying out will all play a part in your eventual success or failure.

One of my first purchases in the early spring is Alyssum maritimum – which should perhaps be in the self-seeding section. The small white Alyssum which smells of honey is a widely sold annual but that detracts not a jot from its charm both to human beings and bees. It has a special nostalgic attraction for me; when I was a child at the end of the last war, my parents' house received a direct hit from a bomb and was completely destroyed. After drifting from one depressing, rented house to another, we were lent a gardener's cottage on an estate at Stanmore in Middlesex. The garden path was self-seeded by mounds of this little white Alyssum during the summer and the heavy smell always means another happy summer to me. I am not so fond of Alyssum saxatile, which is perennial – I find its yellow colouring harsh. A. saxatile citrinum is a good lemon colour, as its name suggests, and has double flowers; they do well in a rockery.

Your Alyssum maritimum may re-seed itself if happy in a sunny position in cracks, in paving and poor soil, but I always buy some more just in case and cram them into every nook and cranny – don't put them into your borders. They will look a little 'planted' for a week or two but then they will settle down and spread in the nicest way, and flower for the rest of the summer.

My next priority on the annual shopping list is the Nicotiana, the sweet-scented tobacco plant. These fragrant plants will flower from July to October in shades of white, green, pink and crimson and are invaluable. There is a 'Dwarf White Bedder', a self-explanatory name, which grows to about one and a half feet high, but the more common plants reach a height of two to three feet high. I have a particular fondness for the green Nicotianas which cool down the bright colours in your summer borders.

Penelope Hobhouse, who gardens the National Trust garden at Tintinhall in Somerset, has generously given me some seed of a species called Nicotiana sylvestris, which was raised for me by a friend. This is a much taller and bigger plant with white flowers that hang in roundels, like the Stephanotis, and is a spectacular flower for the back of a border. It flowers later than the ordinary Nicotiana, and you want to get it well under way in early spring, otherwise it will only begin to flower just before the frosts. You can obtain seed from Thompson & Morgan in Ipswich (Thompson & Morgan, Ipswich, Ltd; London Road, Ipswich, Suffolk; telephone 0473 688588) now, and this is a really glamorous addition to your garden; if you can raise plants from seed by hook or by crook, it is well worth trying, especially as they may, if left in situ, return again the following years. The Nicotianas will flourish in shade as well as in sun, but are more prolific in the sun.

Petunias are happy plants to buy as annuals, and will flourish gaily all summer if you take the minimum amount of trouble to pick off the dead heads every weekend: a not too arduous job which can be delegated to a middle-aged child or a guest wanting to appear helpful. The white ones are very beautiful (except just after rain) but there are colours to suit all tastes, including a deep violet blue which looks magnificent planted underneath lavender.

The wallflower, Cheiranthus, can be treated as an annual and it fills an early gap in the garden as it is hardy and flowers for about a month or so (between February and May). I fill big tubs in the front of our house in the autumn and they produce a profusion of tawny velvet flowers with no problems. By the time these are fading I can safely replant with ivy-leaved geraniums which I overwinter in our conservatory, and which flower through to the first frosts. I do leave one or two wallflower plants in the border and in the walls to survive until the following year. Wallflowers growing out of cracks in walls are most attractive and seem to be quite happy and hardy, hence their name; so do try to establish these. The perennial wallflowers like growing out of a rockery or sunny stony place over stone slabs or paving and I will deal with them separately (see page 89).

I like to plant the dwarf Cheiranthus in our tubs (Erysimum). They are less straggly and bush out more than the large wallflowers, being unaffected by wind.

The only annuals we grow for picking are sweet peas. The other flowers in the garden are too precious to pick unless we have a glut of roses, and so most of the flowers in the house are pot plants from the conservatory, except for sweet peas which produce more flowers if

Lathyrus odoratus (sweet pea)

regularly picked. The smell of a bowl of these is irresistible.

We sometimes grow sweet peas up a large-based pyramid of trellis in a well mulched bed. As early as we can, we buy seedlings at Nine Elms, keep them for a week or so in the frost-free conservatory, and plant them out as early as I dare (March or April, depending on the district). Remember that sweet peas need sun, and for preference not a howling draught, but they are hardy annuals. The Latin name of the normal sweet pea is Lathyrus odoratus and there are many varieties, including a dwarf – 'Cupid' – which only grows about eight inches high. Personally, I feel this dwarfness defeats the object of the well loved sweet pea, but I may be wrong.

While you are thinking of Lathyrus, let your mind dwell on the everlasting pea, a perennial which is a good trouble-free climber: you will find it in the chapter on climbers.

A dear little annual which will re-seed itself if happy in its position is Limnanthes. This charming plant, sometimes known descriptively as the poached egg flower, is about six inches high and thrives in a sunny position with a cool root run; it is ideal in gravel or paving stone cracks, or else in a rockery.

If you would like an annual that is unusual and different, do try to lay your hands on a few Cleome seedlings, or try to find some way of raising them from seed. The Cleome or Spider Flower is a gorgeous herbaceous plant growing, in a sunny spot, to a height of three feet and bearing great heads of pink or white flowers from July to September. The flowers are fragrant and spectacular and come into bloom just when many early summer flowers are fading.

Another really different annual is Molucella, commonly called Bells of Ireland (of course they naturally hail from Syria). They have long spikes of sour-green calyxes, and are extra specially satisfactory for they thrive in all positions, except for deep shade, and look as refreshing as a cool drink in August; they are exotic when picked for a vase and are easy to dry for winter flower arrangements.

These last two annuals are not usually found in nurseries and garden centres but, if you can't manage yourself, you may find a friend to raise a box of seeds to seedlings for you, and you won't regret it. Dried Molucella and dried Anaphalis make an unusually beautiful fresh green and white vase to cheer up a gloomy corner.

PERENNIALS

The backbone of your borders must obviously consist of shrubs and perennials. I won't say that this is completely troublefree gardening, but once having found out what thrives with you, life becomes easier.

I feel that one needs a few sculptural plants in the border to avoid the monotony of plants gently rising from short to tall. We will talk about foliage, and flower colour, interspersed with greys, greens and whites to avoid heaviness on the eye as regards colour; but interesting forms must interrupt your bed to provide interest. I have already suggested Euphorbia wulfenii and here are one or two others which are interesting and within the capabilities of the part-time gardener.

One is the Phormium tenax – the New Zealand flax – a welcome and beautiful import. A word of warning here: this plant can grow very big, and before it gets established can be fragile, but the colours are fascinating and subtle, with bronze or variegated foliage. One grows the Phormium for its swordshaped leaves, but you may achieve a spike of flowers, not really beautiful, but exotic and interesting.

From time to time my mother has given me generous divisions of her Agapanthus, and for the weekend gardener this is the only way to obtain this worthwhile plant. There is no way that one can have the time (or patience) to grow the Agapanthi from seed which takes about five years until it flowers. I fear its childhood would be a sad disaster. However, if you can find a nursery who will sell you mature plants, or, better still, if a kind friend will divide up some of theirs do acquire them. If you live in the north of Britain, you may have doubts about the hardiness of this African lily, but you could always plant them in tubs and move them into a cool greenhouse. Otherwise they should be planted in a sunny, sheltered position and they will flower in August and increase. The Headbourne Hybrids are pretty well hardy and range from a deep blue to a paler hue. I find that the white varieties, though very beautiful and good for picking, are shyer to flower and less hardy, but once established are extremely attractive.

The Astrantia major is a fine perennial and easy to grow with stalking flowers of pale green and pink. Astrantias will grow at least two to three feet high, so are more suitable for the back of the border. Once it is established you can divide it in the autumn. The colouring is soft and the foliage attractive. My plant was divided and given to me by a friend living in the Isle of Skye so I feel this must be a plant which can grow throughout Britain, given a sunny position.

The garden pinks are good, uncomplicated, and provide long-flowering plants for the front of your border with beautiful, subtle colourings and delicate grey-green foliage. They like sun and dislike acid soil, but if you have any chalk or lime in your soil you will have no problems with pinks – Dianthus by name. The larger species is Dianthus allwoodii, a cross between the Dianthus and the perpetual flowering carnation: Doris, Daphne, Diane, D. haematocalyx, Mrs Sinkins (white), Gran's Favourite, and so on are but a few of these pretty pinks and you will find your own favourites. Even the weekend gardener can try to add to their collection by tweaking off non-flowering shoots in the early

Dianthus (pinks)

summer and rooting them in pots of sharp sand plunged into damp peat to prevent them drying out.

Peonies are very good trouble-free, herbaceous plants, needing no special care, and, I believe, can last for about fifty years. The lovely old cottage garden favourite, P. officinalis, flowers earlier than the species (May to June) and can be obtained in three colours, P. 'Alba-Plena', P. 'Rosa-Plena' and P. 'Rubra-Plena', self-explanatory names. They have a blowzy charm, are delightful picked in a vase, and their leaves are attractive too. But if you prefer sheer elegance to blowzy charm, the tree peony cannot fail to tempt you. Tree peonies in a border look stunning the whole summer. Even when brown, their leaves gracefully sway in the breeze with pinky-red veins tracing their way down through the grey-green serrations. Their magnificent blooms are like faded silk crinolines of yellow, pink or white and this spectacular plant is ideal for the weekend gardener, given a well drained position. They need no pruning, spraying or special attention, bar feeding. Worry not if they do not flower for the first year or so – they will if you are patient.

Another delicately sculptural plant is the Dierama pulcherrimum or Wand-flower, also known as angels' fishing rods – names which describe well this large but fragile-looking plant with its long curved 'fishing rods' of white or purple flowers in June or July. The leaves are long and grass-like, and the Dierama likes a good well-drained soil, and a sunny position; it grows from corms. Dieramas are extremely graceful plants which do not take up a lot of room, for their 'fishing rod' flower stalks overhang lower plants without shading them. I would be wary of Dieramas in a very cold northern garden.

Dicentra formosa

Dicentra or Bleeding Heart is a charming and amenable perennial growing cheerfully in the sun or shade which has a really good long flowering season. D. formosa is my favourite for it does not grow high enough to need staking; and its pretty sprays of pink heart-shaped flowers are set off by delicate and feathery foliage. Dicentra spectabilis has a form, 'Alba', which grows in May and June and I am longing to plant lots of it this year. D. eximia is prolific and long flowering, with beautiful grey-green foliage, lasting well into September with pink or white flowers; a plant which really earns its keep.

The Hemerocallis, or Day Lily, is amenable and easy to cultivate, forming large root clumps below the soil. It will be happy in sun or partial shade and needs little fertilizing. Although the flowers last only a day, hence their name, they are replaced by the next bud down the stem over a good long period in mid-summer, especially in August, when the garden can take on that exhausted and spent look before the September flowerers appear. The Hemerocallis grows large (two to three feet), and so is not necessarily a plant to grow in the front of your border. The modern hybrids range in colour from yellow, through the tawny shades, to brick and deep red, and they may be divided in the spring or autumn. A really trouble-free plant.

If you can find it, there is a variegated Hemerocallis which is as pretty in flower as it is either out of the flowering season or in the evening when the flowers are closed. Seize this one if you have the chance.

White Knipophia, the white version of the rather unattractive Red Hot Poker, is a goody, with greeny-white spikes of flowers. It likes a fairly rich soil and a sunny position and may be divided in the spring.

I have acquired two daisy-type plants during this last year, which are new to my garden, and both have flourished like the green bay tree in sunny positions. The first one I planted as quite a small plant in the terrace where there is a two-foot square patch of poor earth that faces due south, but is apt to dry up and get baked dry during the summer. I planted Agathaea coelestis, which grew during the summer into a good clump (two feet by one foot) and bloomed with sky-blue daisy flowers until the late autumn. I am as delighted with this new acquisition as I am with my second, which should really be placed amongst the grey plants. This is Leucanthemum, or Chrysanthemum hosmariense; it makes a small bush about three feet by two feet with shredded grey leaves, and single white yellow-centred daisy flowers about the circumference of a fifty pence piece. I planted this in an east-facing border against a wall which gets the sun from midday onwards, and it was covered in flowers all summer. In the late autumn I trimmed the bush as one would a lavender bush to keep the compact shape. These two are tender and so sadly should not be classed as trouble-free. They are more of a gamble to over-winter, but worth a try, especially in the southern counties or in a sheltered position.

An essential low-growing herbaceous perennial is the Pulmonaria, commonly known as lungwort, or 'soldiers and sailors'. The latter name stems from the fact that the flowers often change from pink to blue. The leaves of P. officinalis are spotted with silver and the whole plant resembles a coarse, enlarged forget-me-not. This being said, it is a loyal friend in any soil. Year after year it appears at primrose time and soldiers (or sailors) on, even in the most disastrous spring. Not the most beautiful, delicate blooms, but profuse and gay – in the original sense of the word, casting no aspersions on the military or naval professions.

Self-Seeding
and Spreading Plants

*H*AVING COVERED THE use of grey and lime-green plants as a foil for the border, we must think of comparatively trouble-free plants to complete your creation. Every gardener will have his favourites and any chapter on mixed border and herbaceous plants will, of necessity, be a personal point of view. Our weekend gardeners can divide their attention between three categories: self-seeding plants, perennials, bedding-out plants. Bulbs and shrubs will be dealt with in another chapter (see page 65).

SELF-SEEDING PLANTS

Self-seeding plants are a joy to the weekender, and every year one greets the old friends who, one hopes, return, as surely as the swallows return to nest under the eaves. It must be admitted that some species dwindle or grow smaller year by year, but it is no great hardship to provide new blood from time to time, and weed out the weakly seedlings to provide fodder for the compost heap.

Poppies do wonderfully in our slightly chalky soil, and in June our borders resemble an opium grove. I remove the undersized seedlings but leave the biggest seed pods, which are attractive in themselves, to ripen and shed their seeds before disposing of the dead plants. Papaver orientale is a regal poppy and will grow to three feet in June in shades of white, pink and crimson. The Shirley poppies, Papaver rhoeas, are attractive in a more delicate way. Papaver somniferum has beautiful grey-green leaves and seed pods, and is a strong poppy, usually capable of standing up to winds and rain without collapsing. Poppy flowers of course only really last one day, but their ephemeral charm is one of the great joys of summer. They are ideal for the weekender to pick for the house. I am told that if you dip the ends of their stalks in boiling water the petals will not fall.

The dear little Welsh poppy will spread itself around your garden happily – I prefer the yellow colour to the harsh orange. I also love the wild common red poppy, and if you have a bit of garden that you like to keep rough, it is easy to scatter a few ripened seed pods in a sunny position. These will give you a week or two of startling beauty and will not overwhelm you as some wild flowers can.

There is no easier friend than the Myosotis, or forget-me-not. Once sown he will renew himself by self-seeding and after he has provided a haze of misty blue, which hides the fading daffodil leaves, you may easily pull him up when he turns mildewy, by which time his seeds will have set, and will be scattered by the very act of removal. I try to take a little more care over the pink or white plants for these are more fugitive, and it is pretty to have a mixture, although the blue will always predominate.

Aquilegias will self-seed prolifically, and they are all charming, springing up between paving stones, and in all sorts of nooks and crannies. These 'Granny's Bonnets' come in all colours but it is worthwhile gathering seed heads of any special colours that you may find in assenting friends' gardens. I have seen beautiful red ones in Dumfriesshire – Aquilegia canadensis – and have high hopes of some pure white ones brought back by a Himalayan expedition.

Do sow or scatter some Love in the mist around your garden. This charming traditional flower (Nigella damascena) will enhance any sunny position during late June and July. The self-sown flowers will become smaller over the years, but may be easily augmented by a fresh supply of seed from time to time. Take a little trouble to examine these flower and seed heads carefully: their architecture is fascinating and the seed pods are like ballet dancers.

Foxgloves will naturalize if happy in their position; the Digitalis likes

49

shade and dry soil. The Excelsior hybrids are beautiful and will re-seed themselves, dying down in the summer. I find that foxgloves usually revert to the purple colour – with the great bonus of a white one occasionally. I do try to plant the lovely soft apricot colours but they only last a couple of years with me. This being said, once you have established foxgloves they will re-appear in varying colours, year after year, and they are a truly spectacular apparition. These are one of those plants which decide where they are happy and then persist in a gallant, proud way and make one corner of your garden their own, without becoming over-invasive.

The Anemone is an adaptable perennial which fills many gaps, and enriches all parts of the garden in various seasons. The genus is so large that I will pick out just a few. Anemone blanda has blue flowers and soft furry leaves, and flowers in early spring. It is fibrous rooted, as are A. appennina and A. nemorosa, and they enjoy a shady position under trees. A. nemorosa, with its white or pink flowers, looks dream-like planted as a mass underneath a big tree. You may have to persevere to get this started, but once established its roots will resist all vicissitudes and it will return every spring to give you great joy. Do not mow if they are planted in a lawn until the leaves have died down, as you would treat daffodils or hyacinths. These pink and white flowers are a refreshing change after all the yellow flowers which abound during the early spring. I planted the white A. coronaria 'de Caen' strain called 'The Bride' this year, and was enchanted by the stark white early flowers brightening up grey days. I shall plant many more next year. A. coronaria and A. fulgens are also spring flowering; from tuberous roots, they can be grown in borders, but I find their vivid colours harsh and strident.

The Japanese anemone, A. hybrida, does not like being moved, but if you can find a good container-grown plant to buy, it will repay the effort of getting it started. Happy in any soil, and especially under a wall, it flowers prolifically during that August gap. It will continue to flower from August to October, and the white-coloured one is refreshing in a hot and dusty garden. One often sees this charming anemone in old cottage gardens, re-appearing year after year, and, once established, it will naturalize.

If you have some corner of the garden where Lilies of the valley will not be disturbed, this plant, Convalleria majalis, will spread and with its delicate fragrance is a joy in May, both when growing or in a vase. The French offer them on May 1st as 'porte-bonheur' to wish each other

Anemone coronaria

good luck. A good spreader for the part-timer, needing no upkeep except for a mulch of manure or compost in February; and its leaves will suppress the weeds to a certain extent.

A one-cover crop, or spreader, that I personally would not plant, unless perhaps I had broad acres a long way away from the house, is the variegated dead nettle – Lamium. It is fashionable at the moment but to my mind many weeds are more attractive: it is invasive. You will have difficulty in ridding yourself of it once it is established; the leaves, though variegated and thickly growing, are drear and the flowers even more so. However, you may think it entrancing – so be it – but if a kind friend offers you a plant, enthusing over its variegated leaves and its yellow/pink/purple or whatever florets, think hard before you plant. (The pink ones are less invasive.) You may be happy to let the Lamium cover your garden, subduing all weeds, and also all precious plants – on your head be it. You may be fashionable for a year or two, but in my mind your garden will have a low boredom threshold in three years.

I find the Ajuga, a relation of the wild bugle, can also be a bit of a

Ajuga reptans 'Burgundy glow'

bully boy as ground cover – with the exception of A. 'Burgundy Glow', an attractive variegated-leaved plant, with vivid blue flowers when in a sunny position, and rather more delicate about its invasions into the border than its bronze-leaved brother.

A new acquisition last year in our border, which has proved a great success, is Convolvulus mauritanicus: its height (three inches) and trailing habit makes it ideal for under-planting or for the front of borders, as long as the site is sunny. The flowers are small but profuse, of a vivid, beautiful blue, and look marvellous against a grey foliage foil. I have planted this spreading plant under roses; I feel that it does not in all probability take out too much nourishment from the soil, given the fact that roses have deeper roots. Rose beds which have bare soil are only too ready to receive weed seeds, and always look so artificial, to my eye.

For spring planting do try to plant the lovely Fritillaria meleagris (the snake's head fritillary) which, if happy, will spread, especially under trees – the white Alba and the purple are really beautiful plants.

Others to try are the dog tooth violet (Erythronium), cowslips, which will re-seed if left to, and of course the Cyclamen. C. hederifolium (sometimes called neapolitanum) flowers from August to November, and C. coum from December to March; also C. persicum which flowers from March to April. These Cyclamen all have beautiful marbled leaves, and will spread and multiply if left in peace. They are mostly in shades varying from white through pink to purple, and are happiest in leaf mould under some tree or shrub where their mounds of dappled leaves, with the bonus of gem-like flowers, are well worth a try. I do try to put a bit of wire netting over the corms when planted, before they ramp away (five to nine inches high), for they are invisible when dormant and can be easily forgotten.

There are some perennials which, once planted and bar what insurance companies are pleased to call an 'Act of God', will almost certainly stay with you forever, re-seeding themselves and popping up all over your garden, summer after summer. I give you a list of the most welcome of these common plants:

Alchemilla mollis
White alyssum
Aquilega (columbine)
Honesty
Nasturtium
Forget-me-not
Love in the mist
Wallflowers
Poppies
Snow in summer (Cerastium tomentosum or C. beibersteinii)
Ajuga 'Burgundy Glow'
Creeping Jenny (Lysimachia nummularia)
Cyclamen
Golden feverfue (Chrysanthemum parthenium aureum)
Centranthus (valerian)

I would bet that, if you wished to bring your gardening down to the minimum and with the most colourful results, a bed of just these plants would achieve this – it would be fun to try. You will probably, by trial and error, be able to add to this list, depending on your particular permutation of soil and situation.

Climbers

*I*F YOUR GARDEN is surrounded by walls you will not only have privacy, you will also have shelter and a whole new dimension of growth. However, do not despair if you are deprived of walls in your garden as you obviously must have, one hopes, at least two walls you can use for climbing plants, that is to say the walls of the house itself. On second thoughts, perhaps, if your house fronts onto a street, you may only have one wall at the back, but roses, honeysuckle, clematis and jasmine are gorgeous when grown up old trees, especially fruit trees. I can hear the dismayed part-timer groan and say, 'But I have no lovely walls, nor old fruit trees – this chapter is not for me.' Not so: a good strong thick stake, sledgehammered into the ground, and topped by a plastic-covered wire framework resembling the skeleton of an umbrella (which you may purchase from a good garden centre) will provide the wherewithal to grow climbers and give a vertical dimension to your garden. This last solution to the climbing problem will look like a bare, bony mushroom for a couple of years, but it is worth persevering for the plants will eventually clothe the framework, and obscure the support, if only you have hope, faith, and charity in the form of manure or fertilizer.

Impossible to know where to start extolling the varieties of trouble-free climbing plants for the weekender, but being one of the first to flower in the spring, the Clematis montana jumps to mind. Given a well prepared site when planted, the C. montana will ramble happily without undue attention. I have planted the white one, which trails over a laurel bush thereby hiding an oil tank. I carefully prune the laurel, a bush which I do not like, but which provides a good prop for the charming montana. I say 'carefully prune', because the Clematis stems are only too easy to cut through by mistake, and it is agony to take off a year's growth with one careless snip. I prefer the white C. montana, having a

Clematis macropetala

passion for white flowers, but I have seen superb swags of the pink version draping themselves over walls, telegraph wires, and anything else which will give them a stable berth. The pink blooms slightly earlier and is, I suspect, rather more prolific.

An excellent book to read on the subject is *Clematis* by Christopher Lloyd (published by Collins), suggesting a Clematis which will be in flower for every month of the year. This is probably a bit over-ambitious for the weekender; also, Clemati are prone to wilt. But the book is a fund of information and usefulness.

Another Clematis I love is the evergreen C. armandii whose leaves are a decoration in themselves, and which flowers at Easter-time. This is a fairly tender Clematis, but worth a try for the benefit not only of its charming blooms, but also for its evergreen and elegant ovate leaves. My other favourite Clemati are the early semi-double lavender C. macropetala, the prolific 'Mrs Cholmondeley', a large-flowered lavender-coloured plant which will flower all summer, and above all, the C. orientalis. C. tangutica is another friend from China which has the same advantage. C. orientalis, the 'lemon peel' Clematis, is not only prolific, and a strong rambler, but also has the benefit of attractive silky seed heads as well as nodding yellow flowers. This is ideal for growing up a wall or an old tree. C. 'Nelly Moser' is, of course, an old favourite, and one of the most prolific in flower-power. She is large-flowered and striped with carmine, and there must be a place somewhere in your garden where you can squeeze her in. Personally I plant all my Clematis with four old roof tiles surrounding their roots. This protects their little stems which look so dead and unassuming during the winter, and are liable to get damaged. It also keeps the ground damp during what one hopes are the hot, dry days but which although pleasant are often a worrying feature of the summer months.

I have seen some Clematis used as ground cover: this can look spectacular, but I feel that the problem of weeds growing up through the scrambling Clematis is too much for the weekend gardener. If you wish to grow Clematis horizontally, a better idea is to let a prolific one meander across a bed of winter flowering heathers, thinking along the lines of having a bed which is attractive twice during the year. The only problem with this planting scheme crops up when you wish to trim the heathers, or to weed.

The first jasmine that one must plant is the Common White Jasmine – 'Jasminum officinale' – by virtue of its undemanding habit of good growth when planted in a sunny position, and its deliciously fragrant clusters of flowers. Because a plant is well known and easy to grow, one must not fall into the trap of thinking that it is not excellent. Only too often plants become fashionable and then decline in popularity because one has seen them in every garden. How much better, especially for the occasional gardener, to have a garden full of fragrance, strong growth, and free-flowering plants, than weedy, rare and obscure speci-

mens. You will *always* have something unusual if you are a gardening
enthusiast, and this will show to advantage against a happy, well grown,
well fed setting of enthusiastic plants. I suppose the only exception is
the house or little cottage with no garden, except for a magnificent
wistaria, or magnolia, but in that case you will have no need for this
book.

I love the pink Jasmine with variegated leaves – J. stephanense. It is
a charming, sweet-smelling Jasmine, but shyer of flowering than the J.
officinale. That being said, I would always try it, and cosset it a little
over the first few years, making sure that it is planted in a good sunny
position; you will be well rewarded. J. nudiflorum, the winter Jasmine,
is a real joy because it provides colour at a bleak time of the year, and
is so good to pick for a vase, giving hope of spring inside the house,
even if the weather is lousy outside. Prune this hard after it has flowered,
and try to grow it up a wall, so that the flowers' spikes shoot down –
they look at their best like this. I find the winter Jasmine looks attractive
during the summer with its lush green foliage, although it flowers in
the winter on bare spikes. I grow Clematis up it; C. 'Mrs Cholmondeley'
is the one happily rambling up my winter Jasmine, but I must try C.
tangutica, or C. orientalis because I think that the two plantings would
make a really good all-round wall covering. J. nudiflorum is easy to
propagate through layering.

Another evergreen Jasmine that I have planted this year is J. revo-
lutum: the foliage is charming and the flowers are large and yellow,
flowering from June to August. The flowers are fragrant, and the only
thing to remember about this Jasmine is that it is non-twining so needs
a little tying up – not a taxing task.

The honeysuckle (Lonicera) is a climber with few peccadilloes and
all the advantages in the world. You have an enormous choice, and as

the honeysuckle can be grown on all soils, given enough moisture and good feeding, you will be well rewarded by fragrance, beauty and happy pollen-sodden bees. I would single out some honeysuckles which, in time, will give you great pleasure: the two Dutch honeysuckles, Lonicera periclymenum – the early L. belgica and the late L. serotina – with their creamy insides and roseate outsides and buds. L. belgica flowers from May to July and serotina from July to September. These two planted together will give you a lovely long flowering season. Lonicera americana is often confused with these; it flowers in June and is, I think, the most vigorous of all. If I were to choose one honeysuckle, I think Americana would be my choice. It is unbelievably prolific in almost any sunny position, and as fragrant as it is beautiful. Do plant this; it is trouble-free and will give you a tremendous display of flowers with very little effort on your part.

Lonicera sempervirens (honeysuckle)

The other honeysuckle which really earns its keep is L. Japonica 'Halliana', for it is nearly evergreen and very fragrant. Given a southern climate, L. 'Halliana' will continue flowering right on into November and past the first frosts. This honeysuckle may not make a great display as late in the year as this, but you can still pick it for a vase – with maybe Viburnum fragrans, winter jasmine and rosehips, and you will have beauty and fragrance to gladden your table on a dull, dark late autumn day.

When I say that L. 'Halliana' carries on well into the autumn, this is not to detract from its prime time in high summer when the prolific flowers will provide you with an overwhelming scent of honey. In all, it is a hardworking and disease-free member of the Lonicera family, requiring very little maintenance, except for sunshine and the usual fertilizing.

Lonicera brownii 'Fuchsiodes' is another lovely honeysuckle, with drooping scarlet fuchsia-like flowers, as its name suggests, flowering primarily in June with a secondary late summer burst. This is an exceptionally beautiful climber and has the advantage of being semi-evergreen. Lonicera sempervirens also produces showers of trumpet-like flowers, is semi-evergreen, with yellow insides to its terracotta trumpets, and flowers from June to August.

Cobea scandens is an annual, occasionally self-seeding in mild, protected situations, but do not be put off by this. If you plant bought-in seedlings in a sunny position in the spring, they will be half way to heaven in a very short time, and will flower profusely, withstanding neglect until the first frosts. Morning Glory (Ipomoea purpurea) and Nasturtiums are two other annuals well worth considering. My husband always pokes a few nasturtium seeds in at the base of our garden walls and they never disappoint us.

Solanum crispum Autumnale

A climber which cannot really be described as trouble-free, due to the fact that it is fairly tender, is the Solanum. If you have a sheltered wall, the Solanum jasminoides 'Album' can look most attractive. S. crispum is more hardy but its mauve colour is less appealing. I would be tempted to give S. jasminoides 'Album' a try, for I have seen many spectacular specimens on a sheltered wall. Given the fact that at least once every decade we suffer a really desperate winter which will decimate even hardy plants, such as climbing roses, it seems to me that it is worthwhile gambling on planting some more delicate souls. Ceanothus, Solanium, Passiflora caerulea (passion flower) and Coronilla glauca may, in our temperate climate, particularly in the south and west of the country, give you many years of joy – especially if you can protect the roots a little during the winter in some fashion. It is always tragic after a particularly hard winter to grieve over seemingly dead twigs, but although you may scratch with your thumb at the bark, hoping for signs of green, do not, I beg, reject anything before June, as some plants can rejuvenate themselves from the roots. If you dig them up, and then find that they may be alive, and so re-plant them, this may well deal them the final shock. Have patience.

We have no Wisterias in our three-year-old garden, but I certainly plan to remedy the omission this year, as soon as I can find a suitable large space. Surely the Wisteria must be the queen of climbers. The fragrance of their grape-shaped blossoms in May and June followed by the delicate green leaves and the bonus of a secondary flowering, make for a magnificent climber, whether free-standing or against a wall. If you add to this the age of some Wisterias with their ancient gnarled trunks, their majesty stands above all others. We have probably all seen marvellous old specimens, such as at Hampton Court, which have developed over centuries – an amazing heirloom to plant for future generations. Maybe we should think further into the future than our instincts, which yearn for instant gardening. In our micro-wave oven, convenience-food orientated society, where instant impact is the ruling factor, let us occasionally give ourselves the satisfaction of passing on a legacy, such as an oak, beech, wisteria, yew or any other slow-growing, long-living monument, in return for the bonuses of all the ready-to-plant garden-centre specimens we enjoy.

Eccremocarpus is another fast grower, only beaten by Cobea scandens, which is just as well as it may be decimated by frosts. E. scaber will clamber up any support on a south or west site from late May onwards, flowering freely from June to October, and clinging with its tendrils onto anything within sight. The orange-red tubular flowers are very decorative. Another climber of similar growth is Tropaeolum peregrinum – the yellow cousin of the Nasturtium family. This is usually grown as a short-lived perennial or annual, and I love its butterfly-like blooms of yellow and its delicate way of clambering gently through a shrub or up a trellis. I grew one last year in a tub on the terrace where Camellia 'Donation' and Meconopsis baileyi poppies are planted. I plant these in a peat-based compost for I love them both and they will not live in my lime soil. By the time the pink Camellia had dropped, the Tropaeolum had started to climb delicately up the Camellia to blend in well with the blue Meconopsis. I always love the Tropaeolum speciosum which grows so well in Scotland with its scarlet swags, but I feel that this one dislikes the south, and I have never had any luck with it. If, however, you live up north, or north of the border or in the north west you may revel in growing this lovely climber. The grass is always greener on the other side of the fence, however, and it may be that you will spurn it, for you know it so well. Gardeners are so often perverse, and rarely satisfied with their lot.

Hydrangea petiolaris is a trusty friend on a north- or east-facing wall and I have dealt with this in the chapter on shade.

The everlasting pea, Lathyrus latifolius, so often found in old cottage gardens, is a charming climber, clambering up anything it can get its tendrils on. Usually its freely-born flowers are a gentle pinky-mauve, but there is a form called 'White Pearl'. I prefer the original pinky plant, as the white can look a little insipid, but I suppose it depends on where you grow this. The everlasting pea flowers from June to September, and, once established, is not deterred by frosts or hard weather, drought, or deluge – a perennial friend.

Bulbs, Trees and Shrubs

*T*HE PLANTING OF bulbs is an essential and not too time-consuming part of the weekend gardener's annual programme, ensuring a labour-saving, versatile display throughout the year. Corms and tubers are equally useful in this respect, and any good bulb catalogue will lead you and your cheque book astray during the grey months when the hibernating gardener becomes so frustrated. It is your prerogative to dream, imagine, choose, and then pay; but in mitigation, I would point out that the more you put into your garden the more pleasure you will receive, and many bulbs, corms and tubers will increase in volume over the years. So, you can kid yourself that you are only investing in the future.

You will want to choose your bulbs yourself, and the catalogues are not short on good descriptions, although some of them are rather over-enthusiastic. Here I have laid out a rough check list of bulbs, corms and tubers, together with planting times so that you can evolve and imagine your brilliant garden from the comfort of your armchair.

JANUARY

Galanthus (snowdrops): best transplanted in flower. January/February. Will naturalize.

Cyclamen: corms planted in August under trees or in rock gardens. Good foliage and lovely dwarf white or pink flowers. Will naturalize. C. coum.

Hyacinthus, indoors: plant in September.

FEBRUARY

Crocus: all sorts of crocus flower in early February and March. Should be planted in September to November. Will naturalize. Yellow, blue and mauve.

Anemone blanda: best in rock garden. Attractive pink, white, mauve. Plant in late summer.

Iris reticulata: (6 inches). Plant in autumn.

MARCH

Anemone coronaria (De Caen): red, purple, blue. Strong colours. Plant September/October.

Narcissus, outside (this family includes daffodils, jonquils and narcissi): plant in autumn. Allow leaves to die down in spring before tidying up to provide nourishment for the following year. Do plant 6 inches deep.

Scilla: small vivid blue. Good in rock gardens. Plant in early autumn.

APRIL

Endymion (bluebell): plant in autumn.

Fritillaria meleagris: 12 inches. Plant in autumn.

Fritillaria imperialis: 24 inches. Plant in autumn.

Hyacinth, outside: plant in autumn.

Leucojum (snowflake): plant early autumn in shade.

Tulips: varied types. Plant in late autumn.

MAY

Alliums: all sizes and shapes and colours. Trouble-free. Plant September to October in sunny spots. Plant several bulbs together to make a really worthwhile display. Easy to grow and very decorative. Would be worth three stars in the Michelin Guide.

Erythronium (dog's tooth violet): plant in summer.

Muscari (grape hyacinth): many blues. Plant in late autumn in full sun.

Hyacinths, outdoors: plant 5 inches deep in autumn.

Anemone narcissiflora: white or cream. Lovely against fresh spring green colours.

Tulipa 'Fantasy' (parrot tulip)

JUNE

Xiphium (Iris): plant in early autumn.

Rhizomatous bearded irises: plant in summer.

JULY

Galtonia candicans: 36 inches. Like an enormous white snow-drop. Plant 6 inches deep in March. Very rewarding.

Gladioli: plant March/April.

Lilium: if one over-simplifies, these are divided into basal rooting and stem rooting or rhizomatous bulbs.

Basal Rooting, e.g. Lilium candidum (madonna lily). Plant 2 inches deep in a pot plunged into a plunge bed or else in a border in ordinary compost in full sun in October. Will flower in full fragrant glory in June/July.

Stem Rooting, e.g. Lilium regale. Plant in full sun, ordinary good soil (John Innes) in a pot in a plunge bed or in a border in autumn. Will flower fragrantly in July.

Rhizomatous, American origin, e.g. Bellingham hybrids. Plant in semi-shade, lime-free soil with plenty of leaf-mould in autumn.

Ascertain that your lily bulbs are not lime-haters.

AUGUST

Anemone hybrida: 2 to 3 feet. August to October. White or pink. Plant October to March. Will naturalize.

Anemone hybrida: as above.

Crocosmia (formally known as Montbretia.): be careful as these may try a take-over bid. Will naturalize only too easily.

Crinum (powellii): not hardy except in sheltered places under south- or west-facing walls in the south or west. But do try to be prepared for a year or two's patience – worth a gamble for its beauty.

Colchicum (Autumn crocus): rose, purple or white. Plant in July onwards.

Crocus (autumn flowering): plant from August to September.

Schizostylis (rhizomatous): plant in March in a sunny position. Moist, fertile soil.

Nerine bowdenii: plant 4 inches deep, preferably under a west or south wall in August or April.

Cyclamen neapolitanum: will naturalize. Plant in early autumn with leaf-mould in a well drained soil.

Hyacinth (forced), inside bulbs: plant in August.

Any bulbs which I raise for the house, except for Hippeastrums or Lilies, I stuff the next year along the base of walls in the garden and although they will never have such large blooms again, they naturalize quite happily. Crocuses, hyacinths and jonquils give such joy in the spring that it is a pity to waste a single bulb.

TREES

Assuming that we ignore any trees you have already growing in your garden, we must accept that trees are major decisions when it comes to planting. Obviously they will grow, one hopes, steadily taller and so problems of shade, roots and space must be taken into consideration before the big decisions are made. It is fatal to be too hasty when deciding about tree planting. Shrubs and plants can be moved, but trees are more expensive to change your mind about. The first plea is to remind you that trees that are liable to grow large must not be planted near the house, otherwise you will find your foundations undermined by their roots at a future time when you may be physically or financially unable to deal with the situation.

Remember also that you may wish to spend your retirement in this garden you have nurtured, or else you may want to sell it in ten or fifteen years' time. Will the trees have taken over by then, and, instead of a sunlit lawn with patches of shade, have become a mini-wood? Morbid idea, but worth more than a passing thought when you are beguiled by the ever-tempting garden centre or nursery. If, however, you have inherited a tree which looks as if it may become too large in the future, do think of pollarding it if this solution is suitable. People do not pollard trees in this country nearly so much as on the Continent, and I don't really know why. Trees, pollarded to keep them a reasonable size, and so they don't shut out too much light, can look most attractive. Equally well, a line of pleached limes provide a decorative effect in winter or summer, and a good windbreak.

Having struck fear, or reason, into the heart of the prospective tree planter, let us tentatively proceed. As one has assumed that the garden is small enough to be manageable, the ideal trees are those giving pleasure twice a year with flowers, fruit, autumn colouring, foliage, which is attractive throughout the summer months, or which are evergreen.

It is impossible to list all the trees which satisfy even these stringent specifications, but there are some that stand out immediately although you will, as a staunch individualist, strike out, disagree, and add your own.

Taking the first category of trees with a dual personality, and which will give you pleasure during the spring and the autumn, I would put high up on my list the Prunus and the Malus. The Prunus, or flowering cherry, plum, peach or almond, needs no introduction, and is happy growing on most soils. Forget the heavy candyfloss blossoms of suburban gardens; I am not decrying them, they give me and myriads of others the greatest of pleasure, but I would encourage you to look through, for example, the excellent range presented by *Hillier's Dictionary of Trees and Shrubs,* published by David and Charles, to find an overwhelming choice for every taste, size or shape of garden.

Personally, I love the Japanese cherry 'Ukon', which has greenish-tinged blossom and a good spreading nature, but these trees have so much variety of colour, shape and height that there is one to suit every gardener – it is an agonizing, but enjoyable, decision to make. If you have room, the Prunus subhirtella 'Autumnalis' will give you sheer joy because it will flower from November to March over a period when all is gloom and doom – not beautiful during the rest of the year, but also not overwhelmingly shady, and therefore a delicate addition to your garden. I long, and intend, to plant its cousin, P. subhirtella 'Pendula

Rosea', which is a smallish spring-flowering weeping version in a pinker vein. There are small trees of this family and those with prostrate, weeping or large habits exist in a variety of colours from deep carmine to sparkling white; you must research and discover which is best for your taste and your site – it will be a happy task.

Passing from the Prunus to the Malus (or flowering crab-apple), this is a tree equally suited to all fertile soils, and not only beautiful in flower but in foliage, in autumn colouring and fruit. Most trees flower during April to May and some fruits stay on the trees until Christmas or later – a real bonus.

Again, one is faced with a difficult decision, for there is a choice of flower colour ranging from wine red to cream and white, and berry or fruit colour from brilliant yellow to purple. Again, I recommend you to consult Mr Hillier's Dictionary. I personally have M. hupehensis but his branches are stiff and ascending: I think, given the time over again, I would have chosen a more arching growth, say, M. hillieri. M. 'Golden Hornet' is a beautiful tree, with white flowers in May and a profusion of golden fruits that brighten the grey days of autumn, and remain decorative until the hard frosts when presumably they provide nourishment for the birds. This would be a marvellous present for a golden wedding. If one is following this train of thought, M. lemoinei would be the ideal gift for a ruby wedding. This is literally covered with ruby flowers in April and May, its attractive ovate leaves turn bronze in late summer and autumn, and the fruits are a purple bronze; a tree of great elegance, giving pleasure for most of the year. Both are smallish trees. Yours is the enviable choice.

My third contender for the medium to small tree is the spindle berry and without a doubt I would plant Euonymus 'Red Cascade'. This is a gorgeous tree of medium size, suitable for most soils, especially chalk.

It grows happily in sun or shade, and, although the flowers are insignificant, the autumn colouring is superb; the fat spindle berries of shocking pink that open over golden seeds are prolific and really spectacular, reminding one of the colours of a matador's cloak. This tree is worth every inch of space that you can give it; I am never quite sure whether you should class it as a shrub or a tree but it will not take over your garden or house with its roots or branches and will give you enormous pleasure. Do keep a look-out for blackfly in summer, and spray if you find them or else they will set up a happy and undesirable colony in the leaves.

I must add that there are many other species of Euonymus, evergreen or deciduous, with good foliage, which are very attractive and well worth pursuing – I am only pointing out the one which has done so well for me.

Mulberries are good slow-growing trees to plant, they are happy in all well drained soils, and have an attractive form of growth. The black mulberry, Morus nigra, becomes gnarled with age like an Arthur Rackham illustration, and there is a charming weeping white mulberry, Morus alba 'Pendula', which we are very fond of. Both these mulberries have edible fruit, and I believe the white is the one that silk worms feed on, although, not knowing a silk worm personally, I have never put this to the test. It would be a civilized hobby for one's retirement, though, and a pleasant daydream to imagine oneself happily spinning silken underwear in the shade of a weeping mulberry tree.

Two trees with vivid lime-green foliage which add instant sunshine to any garden, are the Robinia pseudoacacia 'Frisia' and the Gleditsia 'Sunburst'. Both of these, in theory, will grow on any soil but the Robinia I planted was never happy so I have replaced it with Gleditsia, which thrives. This should be no deterrent to those who prefer the

Laburnum alpinum

Robinia Frisia and was probably due to some fault of mine, as one sees magnificent specimens of this lovely tree everywhere. I would put these trees high on the priority list for the sheer beauty of their leaves, which will give pleasure all summer.

Another tree well worth planting for its foliage is the Eucalyptus, which is a very fast grower. There are many different types, usually with soft green-grey foliage, rather the same colour as rue. Often the new leaves are those that are greyer; and as this tree grows quickly it is a good idea to cut branches for flower decoration thus stimulating new growth and keeping the tree from becoming too leggy. E. coccifera and E. niphophila both have attractive dappled bark, and E. parvifolia is chalk tolerant. If you are an impatient gardener, the Eucalyptus will hold great appeal for you because, in a good position, they can put on up to six feet of growth in a year. You may also prune them to any shape required.

There is a decorative sycamore which I would include in this group of trees grown for their foliage, and that is Acer pseudoplatanus 'Brilliantissimum'. This tree is well rounded and, although a slow grower, will thrive on any well drained soil. Its leaves are golden yellow when fully opened, with bronze undersides, but they start on shrimp-pink hands – a lovely and undemanding tree to plant.

A beautiful, smallish silver-leaved tree is the weeping pear, so attractive in the wind. Its name is Pyrus salicifolia 'Pendula', and it will thrive on most soils; it is hardy and a good small tree to plant in either a garden or a courtyard.

The Sorbus family has a lot to offer to all tastes, ranging from the white beams to the rowans, with their diversity of different coloured berries ranging from white, through pink, to orange-red. This 'mountain ash' is indigenous and most members of this family are not only decorative but can adapt to any site or soil.

Before leaving the area of happy trees which you can grow without any worries, one must mention the Laburnum. The larger one, L. alpinum, will grow to a height of twenty feet and the L. anagyroides is a smaller tree, attaining a height of about ten to fifteen feet. There is a version of L. anagyroides called 'Pendulum' which is a weeping tree suitable for a restricted space. All Laburnums will produce a waterfall of yellow, pea-flowers in late May and give you no trouble. Some people dislike them, and one must point out that their seed pods are poisonous if you have young children, but I love their enthusiastic flowering, as a herald of summer. We have two, neither of them intentional. One flourishes in our garden in London, originally used as a stake and now a graceful tree ten feet high, growing in very shallow and poor soil. The other, also once a stake, was stuck in to support our Cytisus battandieri, and took root. Actually, it is really rather a good planting scheme, as as soon as the Laburnum stops flowering, the Cytisus begins and I do love a tree or shrub which obviously says to you, I love it here, let me stay. Very disarming!

People now seem to have a passion for the grey-green Garrya elliptica with its drooping grey catkins. It will thrive in nearly every well drained position and is evergreen and easy to grow, so I proffer it to you. Personally, I find it a no-no; it strikes me as drab, and reminds me of widows' weeds. However, as many people rave over it, you may well care to give it garden room and at least you will feel fashionable.

This is just a brief glimpse into the world of tree planting and I have tried to choose the smaller, more manageable and most decorative trees – just the tip of the iceberg. I would love to be able to have the space and time (and patience), coupled with longevity, to achieve a beautifully planted valley.

SHRUBS

I never know when a tree becomes a shrub, or a shrub becomes a tree; however, there is no need to become too pedantic about it, as all one really needs to know is the approximate size and eventual spread of something before one plants. Inevitably one will have to prune back or remove some trees or shrubs, for a variety of different reasons, but as this is time-consuming, and probably damaging, one wants to limit re-arranging as much as is possible.

One Viburnum, bodnantense 'Dawn', that we inherited in our garden is to my mind definitely large enough to be called a tree, but then it must be very old. I love this Viburnum for the fragrant flowers which start in December, and flower on through the winter; they smell so sweet when picked and brought into the warmth in a vase. Viburnum burkwoodii has the same fragrance with slightly larger flowers and it comes into flower later, around Christmas. Another sweet-smelling Viburnum is V. carlesii 'Diana', a spring-flowering shrub with dark pink buds which open to pale pink flowers. The Viburnum family is large and produces beautiful fruits – for example, V. opulus 'Xanthocarpum' with its great clusters of golden berries, and strangely

Daphne caucasica 'Somerset'

different forms of flowers. The V. opulus 'Sterile' bears snowballs of white flowers and V. plicatum 'Mariessii' has layers of horizontal flowers not unlike a lace cap Hydrangea. Viburnums are happy on all kinds of soil and are not tricky shrubs.

One of my favourite large shrubs is the Cytisus battandieri. This silver-leaved fellow will grow swiftly over twelve feet if placed in a sunny, sheltered position, needing protection in the north. He is not choosy as to soil, and, although deciduous, he drops his leaves very late. The silver foliage shows to advantage in the wind, and the distinctive coneshaped yellow flowers smell strongly and positively of pineapples. This is a shrub which has a lot to offer for nine months of the year, and who could ask for more than that? I do find that it is best to discipline C. battandieri with prudent pruning to retain a good shape, as it grows in a harum-scarum way in every direction if neglected.

If you do not live on a chalky soil, plant Euchryphia, for it is such a beautiful shrub, covered in white flowers during the late summer. I envy all who can grow it. Alas, it is a calcifuge and does not like me. A shrub that likes everyone and who everyone likes, including every butterfly for miles around, is the Buddleia; a happy bush, easy to grow on any soil so long as it is planted in a sunny position. Personally, I do not like the white varieties, like the white Lilac; I find that they look so shabby so quickly, when the ends of the flower spikes turn brown. Since the Buddleias produce flowers over a period of maybe a month, there are always some sad browning flowers which spoil the total effect for me. Neither do I like the harsh yellow Buddleia globosa; this being said, I love all other Buddleias without reservation. You can choose from a variety of colours ranging from lilac-pink through violet to dark purple, and there is a very splendid fellow called 'Black Knight' whose name is self-explanatory. One of the most beautiful, although a little

79

tender, is Buddleia crispa for its leaves are silvery and white on the underneath and its flower spikes are the softest lavender. They are all beautiful and will give you no trouble, except for some severe pruning in the autumn to keep the bush in the shape that you desire.

I have recently invested in a B. alternifolia which has a rather different way of growing – the foot-long panicles of soft, fragrant lilac flowers arch in a weeping fashion, and I hope that this will look spectacular planted on the far side of a rather tumble-down ivy-covered wall, and will droop over it (the ivy is the only thing that holds the wall up). I also hope this Buddleia likes us as much as we like him, but on the whole this shrub thrives in virtually all soils given a sunny position, except for B. crispa which, like all grey-leaved plants, trees and shrubs, is less hardy.

I have seen B. crispa growing at Haddespen in Somerset, under-planted with apple mint on a sheltered wall and it was a delightful combination. Although this book is primarily intended to help the often absent gardener with trouble-free suggestions, I do think that sometimes it is well worth chancing your arm with a calculated risk, if you love a slightly tender plant. I would never try to grow a plant on soil that was unsuitable, but I would occasionally plant, in a sheltered position, something I really loved but which was slightly tender – it is amazing what you can get away with, and the occasional gamble, when it pays off, is very satisfactory.

A shrub for the non-gambler is the Potentilla: an accommodating and prolific flowering shrub, happy on all soils, except very shady and damp positions. These will form charming small dense bushes and will be covered with flowers from May to September, depending on your longitude and latitude. They have a long flowering period everywhere, and must be one of the first priorities for the seeker after trouble-free shrubs. Most Potentillas have yellowish to orange flowers; the choice is large. My favourites are P. Mandchurica, with silver foliage and white flowers, and P. 'Day-Dawn' with flowers of the palest coral. Those people who have doubts about their green fingers can plant this, and relax; and the sunnier the position the more flowers you will have.

Most Acers are happy on any soil except for shallow chalk, and they range from small shrubs to largish trees. You will find one of this family to suit any taste but I venture to pinpoint a spectacular shrub called

Potentilla

Acer palmatum 'Senkaki'. He needs a little shelter from cold winds but will repay your efforts of prudent planting. The branches of Senkaki are brilliant shocking pink, and so are very beautiful even without leaves on dull winter days. The foliage changes from pink when the leaves are opening through soft green in the summer to golden autumn colouring. A dramatic shrub and worthy of a place in your garden, especially if you are fairly lime-free.

The Dissectum group of Acers are well worth your attention. Most of them are small shrubs with deeply toothed leaves, giving a delicate appearance. Their autumn colouring is very effective, ranging through the spectrum from golden to tawny colours and on to vivid red and purple.

A really attractive small shrub (height two to three feet) which will spread is Genista lydia. This has arching, grey-leaved branches, covered in May and June by yellow pea flowers hanging in racemes. By virtue of its growth habit, this broom is happiest on a sunny bank or over-

Rubus tridel

hanging a small wall. The only place where it loses its cheerful demeanour is in heavy soil. G. lydia flowers freely in large hummocks and looks like a patch of sunlight, especially when planted alongside soft grey foliage. The only plea I would make is to avoid planting it near anything mauve; its blooms are of that particular yellow which disagrees violently with the purple shades.

Rubus tridel 'Benenden' is a really amenable shrub, of the raspberry family. It is fast-growing with graceful, arching branches, and bears large blooms, resembling single roses, along the length of each branch in early June. These blooms are like delicate white tissue paper and are shown up to advantage against the fresh green leaves. The flowering season is short but you will enjoy every minute, and this shrub keeps its charm throughout the rest of the year, without becoming heavy and boring like many others.

Exochorda, 'The Bride', planted in a sunny site, will bewitch you in the early spring days with its pure white flowers on arching branches – this is a smallish shrub and looks well in a mixed border. It has the same pure charm as the Philadelphus, and flowers earlier than most shrubs.

The Philadelphus, or mock orange, used to be called Syringa and is a superb, easily grown shrub. It has a graceful habit of growth and in June and July is heavy with white blossom. If you pick the branches for a vase, crush their stems and remove the leaves, you will find that they last well. The only chore to remember when growing the many, equally beautiful, types of this genus, is to prune back the old wood after flowering. If you neglect this the shrub will become 'leggy'.

P. lemoinei has many named hybrids of different sizes and shapes. P. coronarius is happy in a shady position, and 'Aureus' has particularly pretty lime-coloured foliage.

The shrub Daphne is a favourite of mine. I remember staying with some friends for Easter and surprisingly enough there were two or three days of glorious weather after an appalling winter. We sat outside on a terrace and the scent of Daphne odora was all pervading. Daphne caucasica 'Somerset' is less scented but hardier, and bears good flowers in May and early June. A most attractive little, four-feet high shrub. One which is equally attractive, and smells divine, is the Daphne blagayana. Plant this in a sunny position and its creamy white scented flowers will delight you in April and May. If the weather is dreary and no-one will exult in this shrub tucked away in your garden, pick it and bring the beauty into your house.

The Mahonia smells and looks good early in the year, but as I assume the occasional gardener has limited space, I would not press you to give house room, or rather garden room, to a shrub which is enjoyable during a month when you might not enjoy it to its fullest; lovely in March/April but horrid and prickly the rest of the year around. If you have a larger garden, you may think differently.

Ceratostigma willmottianum is a dear little border shrub, with brilliant blue flowers in July. Unfortunately it can only be described as half hardy and so is not to be recommended for cold gardens. Our garden in the south west is sheltered, but we have lost this little gem in a recent cold winter. So maybe you will decide, with reason, that the Ceratostigma is not for your garden, but if you care to chance your arm, I wish you well.

Shade and Sun

A BRIEF WORD ABOUT the extremes in a garden which can provide headaches for the often-absent gardener.

To begin with, many gardens have places which scarcely ever get the sun and these can so easily look dismal. If you have a wall to which this applies, I would suggest Hydrangea petiolaris, a self-clinging hydrangea which thrives on a north or east wall, a tough climber, and quite happy to look after itself. The variegated ivies have no need of sun and can lighten up a dull corner, so long as you don't let them make a take-over bid.

Cyclamen coum seem happiest when they are planted underneath shrubs or trees and have no need of direct sunlight. They are such satisfactory little fellows and will, if they like you, make attractive mounds of variegated leaves. Both C. coum and C. persicum should be planted in a humus-rich soil in summer with an adequate covering of leaf mould, and forgotten about. They will suddenly appear and brighten up the darkest days of November, continuing through until the late spring.

Helleborus niger, the Christmas Rose, is another shade-lover to enliven the winter months. Indeed, most Hellebores thrive in shade, given adequate humus; and Lenten roses, H. orientalis and H. guttatus will bloom until April, while H. atrorubens may be in flower before Christmas. A highly worthwhile family to encourage in a shady spot.

Solomon's Seal and Lilies of the valley are both happier in the shade and once established are both beautiful and amenable. As for the summer-flowering shade-lovers, I would nominate the much maligned Busy Lizzie (Impatiens), and the Periwinkle (Vinca) with Bergenia for the spring. Bergenia cordifolia will flower early on any soil, and the Periwinkle will take over during the summer. The Busy Lizzie is an annual, but it will bravely blossom in the shade, enlivening dark corners the whole summer. There are endless different varieties with an enormous choice of colour; do not scorn it.

I have mentioned elsewhere (see page 24) the hardy Geraniums, several of which like the shade and are happy in any well drained soil. Of the many, I would pick out G. 'Johnson's Blue' which will become a mound about fifteen inches by twelve inches, G. 'Kashmir White' which is slightly smaller, and G. endressii 'A.T. Johnson', with soft pink flowers. These are only three of a very large family, rich in variety, colour and size.

Iris innominata (Californian irises)

Symphoricarpus are amenable shrubs, and although the variegated form, S. 'Variegatus', should be planted in a sunny position, the
snowberry, S. albus, will be quite happy in the shade. The flowers are
insignificant but the round, white, marble-size berries are fun, and
provide interest during the autumn. You can multiply this shrub by
lifting its suckers, which are rooted, and popping them in a pot, or in
another spot. There is another version which bears pink berries, called
S. orbiculatus.

Bulbs will complete your colourful corner of shade (see page 65).

These are only a few of the shade-tolerant or indeed shade-loving
plants – there is no need to endure a dismal corner of the garden due
to lack of sun.

The reverse side of the coin is the problem of the corner of the garden
which is in direct sun, and probably bakes hard and dry in the summer
when you cannot be there to water it. I proffer a few suggestions. If
you have a wall, I would plant the lovely Campsis that one sees in so
many Mediterranean gardens. Campsis radicans is virtually self-clinging
and, given a good hot summer, will droop with soft orange trumpet
flowers. Have patience, for it takes a year or two to establish itself, but
is well worth waiting for. Buddleia crispa is ideal for a hot, dry position
and is the loveliest of the Buddleias with its grey-white felt leaves and
soft lilac flowers, so attractive to butterflies. All Buddleias will thrive
on dry soil and will Buddle away happily on sun and very little earth,
nourished by the love given to them by the butterflies.

If you have room in your sun-baked plot, I would plant an artichoke
or two – they are dignified in a sculptural way and have the advantage
of being as magnificent to eat as to look at. In the wall in our garden
grows a Cotoneaster, with no visible means of nourishment, and,
because of this I suppose, it has never grown too big and produces

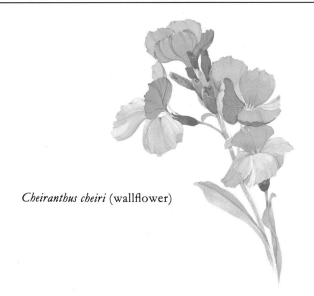

Cheiranthus cheiri (wallflower)

delightful red berries in the autumn. How it survives and on what, is a miracle, but it seems as happy as a sandboy. Also in the crevices of the wall grow wallflowers, happily existing on thin air, or so it seems.

Another 'liver on thin air' in a wall is the old house leek (Sempervivum): if you can plead for one or two of these from friends and stuff them into crannies of walls or roofs with the help of some soil which will stay put in the niche you will find – given a sunny aspect, preferably a south- or west-facing wall – that the so-called leek will proliferate and send out babies. Their leaves become bronze and red with the baking of the sun and they are great embellishments on a grey stone wall. I am told that their phallic flower shoots will ward off thunder and lightning, and if you believe that you will believe anything.

Have patience, and within a year or two you will be well satisfied with this trouble-free planting. It is a pretty sight to see a house leek in mid-summer, with its rosettes tinted red by the sun, and a trellis work of cobwebs sprinkled by dew. If you can find Sempervivum tectorum 'Silverine', it has silvery rosettes which are most attractive. These plants are ideal for shallow urns and stone sinks, where the earth dries up in the summer, as well as for cracks in pavements, but all these Sempervivums develop into families of little rosettes which send out flower spikes in hot summer. They are succulent and evergreen although some of them may suffer with extreme frost. They are very easy to

Eryngium

propagate by tucking offshoots into damp earth or sticking them into a glass of water until roots grow and then planting in compost.

I would underplant the hypothetical sunbaked spot with Sedums, Alliums and Iris pallida 'Variegata'. This Iris has the most beautiful foliage – its spikey leaves of palest blue-green and cream are a joy throughout the year, even when it is not in flower. Remember that irises like their rhizomes baked by the sun (one knows the feeling) so do not plant them deep.

There are an enormous variety of Sedums, all capable of surviving drought and starvation by virtue of their fleshy leaves in which they store moisture, camel-like. S. spectabile 'Autumn Joy' is one of the best; its copper-coloured seed heads are attractive during the winter. 'Variegatum' is another worth growing, with rosettes of green and white leaves suffused with starry pink flowers. There are so many of this family that it would repay you to look around other gardens for those that appeal to your taste. The Alliums are ornamental onions, and both their flowers and their seed heads are lovely. They thrive in poor conditions and are an equally large family. Some are tall and graceful and others quite short; my favourites are A. aflatunense, a tall lilac-headed ball of flowers, blooming in May, and A. flavum, which has pale grey clumps of foliage and bell-like lemon flowers. The sun-baked spot can be improved greatly by digging in stable manure, and although all these plants are undemanding, they will flourish with the help of a little care and mulching.

A new addition to our garden in a south facing border is A. azureum – a small Allium with the most beautiful blue flower head flowering in June. (These Alliums die down completely in winter but if happily situated in a sunny spot will spread.) You need to plant a mass of these bulbs together: it looks stingy to grow them too far apart.

The perennial wallflower, correctly known as Erysimum, is content with poor, well-drained soil, preferably at the front of a border where it can lay its heads on sun-warmed stone. E. alpinum has sulpher yellow flowers produced in May. 'K. Elmhurst' is a sub-shrub with mauve flowers, and 'Moonlight' bears primrose-coloured flowers.

If you have a sheltered south wall and live in the south, do have a try at growing a Romneya coulteri: this is tender and not always easy to start, as it does not like its roots being disturbed. But if you can find a friend or nursery who will give you a well rooted plant, you may be lucky if you transplant in late spring and cover with straw or bracken during the first winters. This is one of those beautiful flowers – a large white 'tissue paper' poppy with elegant grey-green leaves – that will repay any trouble spent on it, and which, once established, is not pernickety. The only difficulty is finding a well rooted plant and setting it in a good, sheltered position. When this has been done and you have cosseted it a bit during its youth, I find that the lovely Romneya spreads. Each flower (July to September) is a joy in itself, and well worth the effort. After a very hard winter recently, I assumed that I had lost my Romneyas but they re-appeared late and not only re-started from the roots, but they had produced offsprings as well. The gardening experts advise you to cut them down low in October, but personally I leave their long stems on until March, when I prune them, to protect the hearts. They will then spring in the spring, and produce shoots four to six feet high which may have to be staked against winds before coming into bloom. This is *not* an easy plant but once it is established can become one, in the south. You should incorporate plenty of humus (compost, leaf mould, and so on) in the bed before you plant.

Roses

ROSES MUST BE regarded as one of God's great creations, inspiring poets and artists, and lifting the spirits of everyone of us above the humdrum. Even the most reactionary male may wear a rose in his button-hole, or send a posy of roses to a special person, and the loveliest vase on a table must surely be a bowl of freshly picked garden rose blooms of random colours. Curtailing this lyrical train of thought, I would point out that the growing of roses is a thorny, contentious, and very personal matter. This being said, I can only state my opinion, at which the experts and landscape gardeners will roar with laughter and critically point out the pitfalls, while I hope their guffaws will send them reeling into their thorny, well-tended beds.

Personally, I dislike seeing these beautiful plants regimented into the traditional 'rose bed', with bare earth underneath and hard-pruned branches, giving no pleasure for over half a year. What a waste of growing space. Do you really want to devote a 'bed' to Hybrid Teas, with hardly more than one flowering and standing ready to receive weeds with open arms? It may be that the blooms, given this specialist treatment, will be of a superb quality, but to my mind there is no room for this kind of gardening in our hypothetical weekend garden.

How much lovelier are roses that droop with blossoms the whole summer, in borders that complement them with flowers and foliage; roses which ramble over walls and fences, hang from trees which they have scrambled up, clamber up brick and stone and pour themselves over outhouse roofs; roses which stand proudly as mature bushes, grace pergolas and arches, or gracefully clothe a tree stump. The weekend gardener may disregard the 'rose bed' and indulge himself with rosaholic dreams.

Since I have decided that the subject of roses is intensely personal, I will tell you of the ones that have done well for me. The first rose that we planted in our garden was Rosa rubrifolia, now re-named glauca, which is trouble-free, free-standing, and as elegant in foliage as in flower. The leaves are an attractive grey-blue with a purple sheen, and the flowers are single, simple, pink. The branches arch gracefully above any border, framing it but not shading it. I have never had any trouble with greenfly or blackspot on this rose; I love it, and would put it high up on my list of priorities. It also bears the most attractive hips in autumn, so dead-heading is to be discouraged.

My second favourite as a border-planted rose in our garden is 'Buff Beauty', a hybrid musk. This is a pale buff-apricot rose of great beauty, which will re-flower if dead-headed. The leaves are a shiny dark green, and the blooms, which are double, have a delicate fragrance. A bowl of 'Buff Beauty' has an old-fashioned charm reminiscent of parchment and warm candlelight. How beautiful 'Buff Beauty' looks against stone. We spent a recent weekend in the Cotswolds, and the gardens there were sodden with roses. By far the most attractive combination was 'Buff Beauty', against the lovely mellow Cotswold stone. There is something about this prolific rose which brings out the subtle colours in stone, whether the building is a cottage, barn or mansion.

The third rose to be planted, or rather transplanted, in our garden, is also a must for me. This is rugosa 'Alba', the White Rose of York. We uprooted this one in mid-summer when we moved from our cottage to the house where we now live, and replanted it quickly, but with apprehension. Amazingly, it has flourished and we love it dearly. It stands free and firm in all its glory, giving us the joy of fresh green leaves, beautiful folded buds, enormous paper white, golden-stemmed flowers, and magnificent hips, throughout the summer and autumn. I can find no defect in this rose; greenfly and blackspot seem un-known to it; its thorns are ferocious, but one cannot blame it for that.

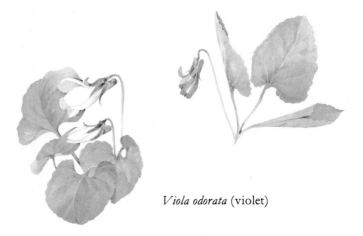

Viola odorata (violet)

The most exciting roses that I have planted recently have come from David Austin. He calls these 'New English Roses', and if one is a rose lover one is apt to become over-enthusiastic and carried away when trying to describe them. Basically they have been bred by David Austin to combine modern recurrent flowering qualities with the characteristic formation and fragrant charm of the old-fashioned rose. Leander (apricot), Charles Austin (apricot and yellow) and Fair Bianca (white) are my favourites, but who could resist a name like Immortal Juno (pink).

Moving on from roses growing in the border, or free-standing, to the climbers and ramblers, the part-time gardener can indulge in more flights of fancy. Let us start off quite gently with Rosa hugonis, which will grow prettily up a wall or in a border. Its branches arch gracefully and its leaves are small, pinnate and decorative in themselves. Single yellow flowers are freely borne followed by good dark hips in autumn – a delightful rose, whether grown as a shrub, or border rose, or against a wall, with that rare combination of delicate yet sturdy elegance.

Progressing slowly upwards and onwards, I would point out three roses which we inherited in our garden – none the less good although not in fashion at the moment. 'American Pillar' is an extremely vigorous rambler in all situations, and used to be a great favourite at the beginning of this century: it flowers only once, but it has quite a long flowering season. I would plant it at the far end of the garden; that is not meant to be derogatory, but rather the opposite. This sturdy rose freely showering forth single pink blooms will need little encouragement and care, will stand any amount of neglect and will draw you down to the end of your garden. I find that severe pruning, when you feel energetic, rejuvenates this rose.

'New Dawn' was another climbing rose we inherited and I find this one has great charm. It grows vigorously and bears small scented double flowers of pale pink, fading to paler pink, throughout the summer.

The last inherited rose I love best of all, although it has only a sparse second flowering. This is 'Albertine', which spreadeagles across the front of our house. Twice it has been cut back to its roots for building reasons, and has returned to the height of approximately eighteen feet again. Do not despair if you have to resort to draconian treatment with your roses on the house; *you* may suffer agonies but I think that many roses are revitalized by severe treatment if it is carried out during the winter months. I love Albertine, despite its tendency to have terrible blackspot on its leaves, for the profusion of copper-pink buds opening into sweet-smelling buff pink blooms which look marvellous against brick or stone. Our Albertine grows up the house, but I have seen good specimens on trellises or pergolas equally happy, and perhaps less prone to blackspot.

We have also inherited two ancient roses: a sweet briar and two moss roses; because they are so well established and prolific, I am very fond of them, although I am not quite sure of their exact names. The sweet briar bears beautiful hips in the autumn and is extremely vigorous, but I would not willingly re-plant another moss rose in the garden for although they are covered with blooms in June and July, they are very prone to blackspot and mildew in August. This may, of course, be due to my particular situation and perhaps I should persevere with more regular spraying with systemic fungicide. I am in two minds about this species for while in autumn I am exasperated by their vulnerability to disease, they none the less amaze one by their spurts of growth and abundance of bloom every year. The fault may lie with me and my lack of time, as a weekend gardener, to give them enough loving care. Blackspot does not seem to dismay these roses – it just looks unattractive in late summer.

There are, in addition to these, some mega-vigorous climbers, which can be spectular in growth. I would like to paint you a picture of a display that I saw last summer in Yorkshire. This was in the garden of a classical, so-called stately home. At the corners of a lawn, preceded by over-flowing herbaceous borders, stood two enormous cedar trees of great age and height. Beyond them a ha-ha leading the eye to uninterrupted views of parkland and distant hills. Growing up these two cedars were 'Bobby James' and the 'Rambling Rector'. On the late June day that we visited this garden these roses were hanging in enormous cascades, shown up by the dark green background of the cedars, up to a height of, I would imagine, at least sixty feet. It was the most amazing, magical sight, almost theatrical in its impact. We lesser mortals will not have the same setting for this idyllic and grandiose planting, but it could inspire someone.

R. filipes 'Kiftsgate' is surely the most vigorous of climbers, and the most prolific with its scented white trusses. The 'Rambling Rector' runs it a close second, and 'Bobby James' is another worthy contender for the climbing rose Derby. These are all white roses, but if your taste bears towards the more mellow range of colours, 'Wedding Day' is a very fine creamy scrambler and 'Maigold' a good scented yellow, which will re-flower if dead-headed.

When we moved into our house three years ago, we found in the long neglected garden an ancient and enormous bay tree, a bush, rather than a tree. This was, or rather, is about eight to nine feet in height and circumference, and looked heavy, large and sombre with its dark green foliage, rather too close to the kitchen windows. We pruned it back as hard as we could but there was no way that we could bring in a bulldozer to excavate the tree, without destroying a wall and part of the small terrace. We searched around for a solution to our problem and came up with an idea which so far seems to have proved successful. Having pruned back as hard as we could, we planted climbing roses around the

Hips of *Rosa rugosa 'Alba'*

bush, and within two years it has transformed the large gloomy, bulky mass into a gorgeous, enormous rose bush with the bay tree still thriving. We planted Wedding Day, François Juranville (fawn pink and fragrant) and Mme. Alfred Carrière (recurrent flowering, pale pink and sweetly scented). These three cover the dark bush and give pleasure throughout the summer months. I tell this little tale to illustrate a solution to one of the many problems which present themselves.

There are two further roses for which I have a great fondness, given the right planting site. They are both ground-cover roses which have the disadvantage, due to their prostrate growth, of being difficult and painful to weed around, but in a terrace bed or wherever you, in your

Primula auricula

wisdom, judge best, they can be delightful. Nozomi is a splendid little rose with single pink flowers and little fairylike darker pink buds. Snow Carpet is equally delicate and charming, from the David Austin stable. He is white, as his name suggests, and also prostrate. Despite what I have said, I have planted him in a bed under a standard white rose and at the moment have steeled myself to suffer pricked fingers for the sake of achieving the effect I want – watch this space, as they say.

Going smaller and smaller like Alice in Wonderland, we can descend to the miniature rose. Do not scorn these minuscule persons: they can embellish sinks, tubs and places where, like the beer, other roses cannot reach. For instance, we have several growing around an old tree stump, and one which has developed into a spectacular big, little bush in a rockery. From afar they look rather mingy; close to, they have great beauty. Therefore, they must be planted in a position where they are close to the eye. I have found that the majority are sturdy, prolific, and repeat-flower over a long season. Not an all-important addition to the weekend garden, but worthy of mention.

I begin to have a real passion for the few striped roses. I am trying to think why, and I suppose that they have an innocent elegance, and are reminiscent of Dutch flower paintings. Rosa Mundi of the Gallica family is a semi-double rose of great beauty, palest pink streaked with crimson. It bears good hips in the autumn, so it is worth your while to restrain yourself from dead-heading it. 'York and Lancaster' has pink and white petals, not truly striped, but with a wayward, untidy, faded charm and truly fragrant. 'Festival Fanfare' is very striking and elegant; a floribunda, it is described by Harkness the rose breeders as 'pale vermilion with creamy white stripes'. 'Ferdinand Pichard', striped pink and purple, is a richly scented Hybrid Perpetual rose. If you can bear to pick your striped roses, a bowl of blooms is the prettiest sight.

Our average weekend gardener does not have a limitless purse to transform this hypothetical oasis into a perfect Garden of Eden. If this was so, gardeners would be employed. He, or she, must come to terms with individual problems in a way that provides the most pleasure aesthetically, with the least hassle. In practically any soil, roses are not really demanding plants, apart from in water-logged, sunless sites. You will have enough time to prune them in the spring, having given them a light 'going over' in autumn. I don't prune severely in the autumn for fear of stimulating weak growth at that season. I do mulch with good, well-rotted farmyard manure during the winter: there is time then for this rather heavy task, that tends to get skimped in spring, but in winter gets the circulation going and gives one the impression of doing good deeds. The frosts will break down the mulch, and one hopes that the earthworms will aid and abet one in the spring by drawing down the goodness to the deep roots of the roses. Some of the goodness may be leeched out but, all in all, the rose will benefit.

For the details of pruning you will find advice in any gardening manual; this book is not meant to be strong on expertise, but rather an attempt to stimulate ideas. I would read those books thoroughly, and then, having digested them, do exactly what you want to do.

As I draw this chapter on roses to an end, I am aware of the enormous choice and the vast range of personal preferences, not to mention the varieties of soil and aspect. Yours is the choice, and what a choice you are blessed with. I have not mentioned 'Zepherine Drouin', the old thornless rose ... the choice is endless and each summer I am tempted afresh, with delightfully agonizing decisions to be made all over again.

Conservatory, Greenhouse, or Windowsill

A CONSERVATORY IS perhaps a grand name for the little greenhouse tacked on to the side of our drawing room, but since I regard a greenhouse as a functional edifice, and a conservatory as principally for display, the conservatory is what we call it and the name has stuck. My mother-in-law calls her conservatory 'the Folly' and she may well be right. We are lucky that our conservatory faces north, and only gets a little evening sun, therefore it does not dry out during the week. You may be able to achieve the same effect by shading – where there is a will there is a way – but you will forfeit the light which is what your plants love. I keep the pot plants standing in deep saucers, or peat, and during the hot summer months I water them on Sunday until the saucers are full, and then I find the plants I keep will be happy until the following weekend. I can hear expert gardeners drawing in their breath at the idea of leaving pots standing in water, but if a plant cannot survive this rough and ready treatment, then I cannot give it house room. The following plants thrive like this and you may find others that will.

Our conservatory has two spotlights on swivel fixtures, so that one can spotlight the plant that is in flower at the moment and appreciate it during the evenings. We also have a thermostatic greenhouse fan heater; I find this an inexpensive way to keep the conservatory frost free and prevent it damping off. The fan re-circulates the air, as well as the heat which would otherwise rise to the roof and be lost through the glass. With a bit of experimentation with the thermostat, depending on the size and aspect of your greenhouse or conservatory and whether it is backed onto the house or not, you can set the dial so that the fan continues, but the heat is only turned on when the temperature drops below freezing point. The mere re-circulation of the air is not expensive in terms of electricity consumption; it is only the heating that adds substantially to the bills. I believe this is the simplest and most econ-omical method of keeping a frost-free, healthy conservatory. We only plug this appliance in during the months when the temperature may drop below freezing.

There are of course other forms of heating, but I believe for the absentee householder they are either less safe, or more expensive, or will dry your plants up too much when you are not there to ventilate or regulate.

The supreme contender for a place in this kind of conservatory is the geranium. Perversely, what you and I commonly call geraniums are really called zonal or ivy-leaved Pelargoniums and we will deal with those. The Regal Pelargoniums are beautiful but they only flower once as opposed to the others which will continue to flower the whole summer, and intermittently in a light, frost-free conservatory for most of the year. So, you must ask yourself, do you have the time and patience to tend the Regals for the benefit of a month's flowering? Not me, so I pass on.

I don't cut down the zonals in the autumn, and so they grow into small trees. These have to be tied and staked but I use the leggy or broken off stalks as cuttings. I do this in two ways: if I have time I slice the stalk diagonally under a leaf, on a good strong shoot, remove the lower leaves, dip the bottom into hormone rooting powder and plant in a good compost mixed with sand. I find putting a plastic bag with an elastic band around the pot causes mould to develop, but I know that many people do this. I feel there is no need, because with a good watering once a week, with the pots standing in a tray under staging in a conservatory, the pots will have enough humidity and they won't dry out. Method two is not so certain, but neither is your time as a part-time gardener – so if I damage or knock off a geranium branch for some reason and have no time, I just put it in a jug of water and hope that it will root in the fullness of time. I would think that I have about a seventy-five per cent success rate.

Pelargoniums thrive in good light or sun, and are a blessing for the weekender as they hate being over-watered. If you pick off all the yellowed leaves and dead heads they will thrive on very little attention and a weekly watering. From very early spring I add Phostrogen to the weekly water, and spray with a weak solution of an insecticide like Malathion at the first sign of insect eggs.

Repotting is essential if you wish your Pelargoniums to grow really big, but be careful not to over-pot them too quickly. It is a matter of finding the happy medium between giving them too much root room, and yet enough damp soil to last from one weekend to another. It is best to err on the dry side, especially during the winter months, and even during the summer. Pelargoniums will not suffer for being dried out for several days. This is an immense family and I am always finding new members, often at local fêtes or plant sales.

It seems that geranium breeders have a penchant for naming varieties after their loved ones. I wonder who 'Granny Hewitt' was, and were 'Mrs Dumbrill', 'Mrs Smith', 'Madame Margot' and 'Mrs Martin' wives, mistresses, or worthy souls that some devoted gardener admired? One imagines a kind of cocktail party in Heaven with these good ladies exchanging petal talk with 'Frank Heatherley', 'Charles Turner' and the rather sinister 'Dr Chippault'; there is even a miniature ivy-leaved fellow called 'Pink Gay Baby'. The only geraniums that I dislike are those with bronze, cream and green leaves like tartan. So 'Maréchal MacMahon' and 'Mrs Henry Cox' can tricolour off as far as I am concerned.

The ivy-leaved Pelargonium is attractive with its hanging growth, and two of the most vigorous and attractive are the plants I know as

Pelargonium 'Reine des balcons' (geranium)

'Roi des Balcons' and 'Reine des Balcons'. Throughout France you will see them dripping from balconies, and they start off deep pink and fade charmingly in the sun so you get a splendid display which is not too uniform and harsh. These are the local French names for these prolific ivy-leaved Pelargoniums, but you will find similar varieties. I believe they are P. peltatum hybrids and I have seen names such as P. 'La France' (mauve), P. 'Ville de Paris' (salmon), and P. 'Galilee' (pink). P. 'Mexicanerin' is red with a white edge. Two other amusing ones, in terms of their foliage, are P. 'Crocodile' which has white-veined leaves and pink flowers, and P. 'L'Elégante' with its white and purple veined flowers and cream-edged foliage, sometimes turning pink in the sunlight.

I use this Pelargonium in tubs on the stone terrace in front of our house and lift them in October to over-winter in the conservatory. I trim them back a bit, really more to save precious space than to make them bush out, and store them under the staging in pots without saucers after watering them well. I then forget about them, except for slurping

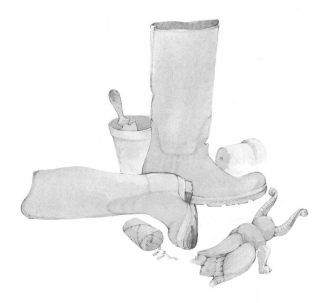

a little water over them not more frequently than once a month. These will hibernate, ready to be brought out in early spring when I begin to feed them, taking off the dead leaves and giving them more light. These are planted out in my tubs when I have lifted the wallflowers in late May. This treatment is different from that given to the display Pelargoniums which stay in the conservatory throughout the twelve months, and so diligently earn their living by providing colour and foliage all year. These hardworking souls must be nourished more often, but do cut down on the watering during the winter or you will get mould on them.

The fragrant-leaved Pelargoniums are as easy and undemanding to grow as the others. The experts will cringe if I say that they thrive on neglect, but their needs are simple. Their flowers are small and, frankly, boring, but their fragrance repays the minimal amount of care they need, and – just a suggestion – what nicer plant to put in a bathroom or loo. P. tomentosum has a delicious smell of peppermint and soft velvety leaves while P. graveolens is not so pretty but smells of lemons.

Quite my favourite plant in the conservatory is a Plumbago (P. capensis). It is an old friend and started off as a fairly small one, on the sunny windowsill in London. Within two years it had grown large and was slowly driving my husband into premature middle-age, for during the summer school holidays when I was in the country during the week, it was in full flower and needed a lot of watering. Our telephone calls usually started off with an anxious, 'Have you watered the Plumbago?' and eventually he went on strike. We then transported it down to Dorset to avoid divorce, and I have re-potted it several times. Now, pruned so that it is tied back to the wall, it can just exist during the summer months if I soak and feed it on Sundays so that it stands with the water up to the brim of the saucer.

If you can achieve this sort of compromise with your Plumbago it will reward you with prolific powder-blue showers of beautiful flowers. In our centrally heated London house it was evergreen, but in the cold but frost-free conservatory it does drop some of its leaves during the winter, or rather they curl up and go brown in an unattractive way. Worry not, this will give you heart to be really callous and prune. Come the spring, just when you wonder whether it is dead, the new growth will start to appear and by mid-summer you will be in business. There is no need to water extravagantly during its dormant months; it only needs plentiful watering and fertilizing during its season of growth and flowering. I love the Plumbago and find its plentiful and graceful flowers and its fresh green foliage a strange combination of exotic gentleness. I hope that you may find it as satisfactory a plant for a weekender as I do.

The Jasmine (Jasminum polyanthum) ranks amongst my three top of the pops, with Pelargoniums and Plumbago, for the oft-unattended conservatory. Given fertilizer, adequate water and good light, Jasmine will grow into a spectacular pot bush and when in flower will smell your house out during the early spring. I find that they put on a great spurt of growth during the summer. Some of them I stand outside on the terrace; I think a good idea also is to sink the pots into a border to avoid too many worries with watering. One wants to tuck the flowing sprays back into the main bush, knitting them together to provide a compact shape. In September, give them a look over and nip off the ends of *every* spray, otherwise you will find yourself with a fantastic bush but no flowers, as all its energy will have gone into producing leaves and stalks. This is quite an easy job – again, one which can be done without worry by guests or youngsters with their fingernails. Your next step is then to bring your plants into the conservatory and fertilize well, and you will find that the flower buds will appear between the leaves. They will take a time to open, and they must have good light, but I have managed to achieve some at Christmas, although I admit most of them are at their best from February onwards. What better time to have that heavy, fragrant scent throughout the house to enliven such a dreary month? A trouble-free and undemanding plant which gives enormous pleasure both to the eye and to the nose for nearly six months of the year.

Streptocarpus (Cape primrose)

I always grow one or two Streptocarpus either in the conservatory or on a windowsill. At the moment I seem to have only the blue variety, but I do love the white ones and I am resolved to achieve these too. It is easy enough to take leaf cuttings from them: all you have to do is to take a large leaf, turn it over and cut through its veins. Place the cut side of the leaf down on a wide pot of damp John Innes Compost placed on a saucer of water so that it doesn't dry out, and put it under your staging in the greenhouse or conservatory. This should be done during the summer. If you put a stone on top of the leaf, it will ensure that the cut veins stay in contact with the damp earth. With luck, you will then have a sumptuous bowl of plants which will only need watering once a week. They are ideal as windowsill plants, as they don't drop their leaves during the winter and provide good greenery even when they are not flowering.

I have lately become enthused by growing tender fuchsias in the same manner as the Pelargoniums in the conservatory – there are some really exotic ones which hail from South America, and can be obtained from Clapton Court Nurseries, near Crewkerne in Somerset. Their leaves are large and graceful and their flowers hang in pendant grape-like clusters – exceptionally beautiful plants whose cuttings are easy to root. The five that are the best for me are F. boliviana (ruby-red pendulous corymbs), F. boliviana Luxurians Alba (similar flowers but white with red petticoats), F. corymbiflora (garnet-red showers of flowers), F. fulgens speciosa (pale green leaves and coral coloured 'flower-showers'), and F. 'Thalia' (bronze foliage and orange flowers).

These are all amazing plants to grow, and, given a frost-free environment and plenty of light, are really easy. The only problem is that of whitefly and your answer is to spray with a different spray each week, if these occur; otherwise the little expletive-deleted insects become immune. They lie low on the undersides of the leaves, laying their eggs, and breeding and feeding like fury. These fuchsias' showy showers of flowers are spectacular, like fireworks; your bosom will swell with pride when your visitors say 'oo – ahh'. The only advice is to keep these mega-fuchsias inside, for example, in the greenhouse, conservatory or on a windowsill where they won't become battered by wind or rain. The more normal greenhouse fuchsia are rewarding as well, and you will find a vast choice of shapes and colours to choose from.

The frost-free conservatory is an ideal nursery for bulbs destined for the house during the winter. Do think about the Hippeastrum, often mistakenly called Amaryllis. If you plant these large bulbs, in stages during the autumn, in a mixture of John Innes 2, peat, and well rotted manure, with half the bulb exposed, and in a pot not more than an inch larger than the bulb (quite a fiddly manœuvre as the roots are lengthy), you will be well rewarded from Christmas onwards by four to six regal trumpets on a tall stout stem, sometimes accompanied by strap-shaped leaves. More often than not, a secondary stem will grow from a good bulb, and the flowers last a good three weeks or so. When the bulbs start to shoot, fertilize with Phostrogen in the water, bring them into the warmth and continue to feed until the leaves, which usually are at their most prolific after flowering, start to yellow. Then let them dry

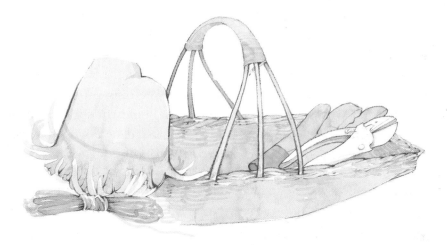

off and rest until the following autumn. Some gardeners may find that the flower heads are too like soldiers on their long stalks, but you can always cut them and put them in a vase; you will find them easy to grow and spectacular, especially during the dreary months. My favourite is called 'Apple Blossom' – a white trumpet tinged with pink, and with a greenish throat, but the corals, reds and striped species cater for most tastes. Jacques Amand Bulbs in London have a marvellous warehouse where you may select enormous Hippeastrum bulbs, as well as lilies, to plant in pots. Their catalogue is mouth-watering, and well worth browsing through for ideas. Their bulbs are also of a very high quality.

One of the real goodies which is a new discovery for me is the hardy perennial, Tolmiea. This form of saxifrage has lime-green variegated leaves which are evergreen. A versatile foliage plant, it is an invaluable back-up plant in borders or pots. You may enjoy it in an unheated or cold room; a bathroom; trailing in a hanging basket or conservatory; or as a ground cover as a foil for bedding plants when its leaves, which rest on the soil, will re-root themselves and self-propagate. The fresh new leaves grow from the mature leaves and so it is variously called the 'piggy back plant' or 'youth-on-age'. This is one of those endearing plants which are so versatile that you will come to depend on it for various reasons. I keep two in the conservatory where, since they are evergreen, they are attractive for twelve months of the year. I bring them into the house to place in front of leggy Hippeastrums, and so on to make a bank of colour when I want a really good display.

Finally, when there is a dearth of indoor plants, the Tolmiea with its vivid, acid-green, variegated foliage stands out in its own right, and is equally attractive in the house or in the border, in tubs or hanging baskets. It has virtually no snags, either in terms of pests or disease, and the only condition it dislikes is a prolonged period in hot central heating – it must not be allowed to dry out. What more can one ask from anyone?

Short Cuts for
the Part-Time Gardener

I
T IS ONLY common sense to bear in mind the technological advantages of the twentieth century, and weigh them up against the old and well tried methods. Each of us weekenders must find our way down this crazy paving, and tread a delicate path between ancient and modern according to our own preferences and timetable. Personally, I feel that nothing can beat a good mulch of compost in the autumn and a spadeful or two of well rotted manure on trees, shrubs and plants. However, when time is short, the new slow-release fertilizers are a boon, especially for tubs and containers. I usually mulch in the autumn instead of the spring, for one has more time then. I know that a lot of the goodness may be leached out of the compost and manure during the winter, but the days are more leisurely than in the spring, when there are always a hundred and one jobs crying out to be done.

Manure must be a year old and well rotted, and even then, of course, one finds that fearful little weeds will appear out of the nice brown mulch after the winter, with warmth and rain, 'poussants petits cris de joie', to tell you that spring and the weeding season is upon you. The part-time gardeners must now forget dreams of arriving at work on a Monday glowing with health and a tan, causing colleagues to enquire jealously if they have returned from some sunny Costa. Rather, they will crawl back to work with a back so painful that it will take until Friday to straighten to a normal vertical position, with hands that are engrained with earth, torn with rose thorns, and nails that are broken, to say nothing of either painful sunburn (only across the back of the neck) or bronchitis, depending on the vagaries of the British climate. His wife or her husband may also be threatening divorce. Is it worth it? How can you ask such a question!

You may find the hardships are alleviated by a mulch of non-weed infected compost, combined with handfuls of Growmore fertilizer, instead of farm or stable manure. From time to time my husband and I rather eccentrically transported our compost buckets backwards and forwards from London to the country, bringing down the vegetable peelings and so on for our compost heap in the garden. This is not so silly as it sounds if you have space in the car, as it is such a waste to throw out dead flowers and peelings and sad salads, when with a little effort and no expense you could be building up a good compost heap. Compost is weed-free so you will also save yourself time from weeding in the summer.

If you can weed and mulch in the autumn you will avoid a lot of trouble during the next year and you will be restoring precious goodness to your soil. You may also think about seaweed as a mulch if you are near the sea. I am told that this, when well composted, is rich in trace elements and humus with the added advantage of being free. Coarse tree bark, commercially sold, and spent hops, or tomato or mushroom compost, are other answers to your mulching quest, but to my mind there is nothing like good home-made compost and it comes free, gratis, and for nothing. Remember that if your friends are having a party or wedding they may be only too happy to let you take away the compostable remains, always remembering that bottles, silver foil and corks won't be of *any* use to your borders. Stick to vegetable matter, sandwiches, and so on, and flowers which will rot down within a year.

So – you have mulched your garden, hoping to keep the weeds at bay. You are not going to stop the weed seeds which are blown in by the winds, but you will stay them. A more severe solution is to weed thoroughly and then spread black sheet plastic, covering it or not with gravel or bark. This is really only practical when making a new bed so that you can then make slits for your new plants which will spread over the plastic. The advantage is that the bed remains weed-free, the roots of the plant remain damp and warm, and you have a low-maintenance border. I feel that it is a synthetic solution, but if you are a sufferer from backache, are elderly, pregnant, or going to be away for long periods, you may find it a solution.

There are no short cuts to the spraying which must be done to guard against greenfly, blackfly, blackspot, and leafcurl on roses, rust on hollyhocks, and all other such blights. If you find yourself on a Sunday, though, with no time or no friendly garden centre open, do remember that diluted washing-up liquid will keep the greenfly away until the next weekend. Diluted Jeyes Fluid will equally well protect the roses against blackspot until you are able to lay your hands on a systemic fungicide. While you are in the mood to spray, remember that Phostrogen is marvellous as a foliar feed as well as a nourishing drink. It is obviously expensive to use on the larger outside garden, and may well be washed off by the next shower of rain before having fed the plant, but the indoor plants will benefit from a phostro-squirt.

To move on from fertilizing and mulching problems to watering: this may be a great headache to the weekend gardener, especially when you have spent money on new trees, shrubs, or plants which have not had time to get their roots well down. Always water really well at a weekend, otherwise a sprinkle does more harm than good, for the roots will grow upwards towards the water rather than downwards where the dampness will usually be found. A sprinkler on the end of a hose pipe is really an essential for you so that watering can go on while you have your hands free for other occupations. However, you may feel that one of the drip-watering systems will solve your problems. These consist of a flexible plastic tubing with emitters, which can be stopped, if necessary, and which will leak water into your borders at pertinent points. This is really labour-saving.

Above all, a garden must be tailored to meet your work capacity – it must be enjoyed not endured. If you are going to be away on lengthy trips in the year to come, or expect a baby, if you are suffering from a back problem, or if you are just growing older, feel no guilt about restricting your garden. If you restrict it to your capability, you may make it a real joy, and you can always expand again as and when you wish: you may want to extend paving and resort to gaps with room for climbing plants, tubs and cracks in the paving for sweet-smelling and spreading plants, all of which will have their roots in the damp and will require little weeding. You may wish to plant more weed-suppressing, low-maintenance shrubs in your borders to cut down on work, or you may feel that putting down part of the garden to wild flowers, bulbs and trees is your answer. Yours is the choice, preferably thought of at least a year in advance. The part-time gardener is, by definition, a hard-pressed enthusiast; the moaner becomes merely a bore. When one

Paeonia suffruticosa (tree paeony)

complains about the weather, time missed from the upkeep of the garden due to weekends away, apologies for weeds, unkempt edges and unmown lawns, one can see the visitor's eyes glazing over. I do *try* not to put on the 'Ruth Draper' act of explaining that the garden was so much better last week when the roses were at their best. A weekend gardener should be supremely egoistical; if you enjoy every moment, every bursting bud and vision of treats to come, as well as joys past, your visitor will see the garden through your eyes, and your enthusiasm will become infectious.

Another side of gardening which must be emphasized is the health aspect. I may be wrong, but I am convinced that dedicated gardeners are healthy in mind and body, and liable to live longer than those with other interests. Not only are they eternally stooping and bending to pluck out an offending weed, or dead head, and therefore taking much more exercise than they imagine, but they are also always looking forward to seeing some plants germinate, come into flower, or simply grow. They are always anticipating the next day, week, month or season and never looking back too much. Therefore they keep themselves naturally aired, exercised and supple, both spiritually and physically. I do seriously believe that those who are psychologically disturbed, as well as those who are recuperating from illness or operations, could benefit enormously by being introduced to gardening as therapy. There is no time in the gardener's day to dwell too long on their own problems as they become so speedily absorbed by overcoming the problems of the garden.

This is not necessarily a solitary occupation, as there is never any lack of fellow enthusiasts who will only too readily suggest remedies, exchange experiences and cuttings, often of doubtful worth but always in good faith.

❦❦❦

Here, finally, is a brief survey list of basic, fairly trouble-free trees, climbers, shrubs, border plants and conservatory plants, month by month. This is only meant to be a rough guide to stimulate your imagination, and encourage research. I have mixed common and Latin names depending on whether the family is indicated (from which you may make your choice) or whether a specific plant is intended. None of these plants is ideal in extreme conditions, and, regarding the conservatory plants, they are intended for a frost-free, rather than heated, conservatory or greenhouse, for example a minimum temperature of 5° centigrade in the winter and a maximum of 22° centigrade in the summer. Calcifuges (lime-haters) are marked with an asterisk*.

JANUARY

Trees Salix alba, Prunus subhirtella 'Autumnalis'

Shrubs Viburnum fragrans, or bodnantense, Mahonia, Hammemalis mollis*

Borders Helleborus niger, Snowdrops, Violets

Conservatory Hippeastrums, Hyacinths, Jasminum polyanthum, Orchids

Climbers Jasminum nudiflorum

FEBRUARY

Trees Willows (Salix)

Shrubs Cornus mas,* Mahonia, Erica carnea*

Border Helleborus niger, Ericas (heathers),* Cyclamen coum, Crocuses, Primroses

Conservatory Jasminum polyanthum, Hippeastrums, Begonia rex, Bilbergia mutans, Hyacinths, Orchids

MARCH

Trees Willows (Salix)

Shrubs Cornus, Camellias, Mahonia, Forsythia, Daphne mezereum

Border Primroses, Daffodils, Wallflowers, Pulmonaria, Bergenia, Erica (heather), Crocus, Polyanthus

Conservatory Jasminum polyanthum, Orchids

Climbers Forsythia suspensa

APRIL

Trees Prunus subhirtella 'Pendula Rosea'

Shrubs Camellia, Forsythia, Daphne mezereum

Border Daffodils, Narcissi, Primulas, Auriculas, Wallflowers, Solomon's Seal, Pulmonaria, Helleborus foetidus

Conservatory Jasminum polyanthum

Climbers Clematis macropetala, Forsythia

123

MAY

Trees Pieris, Prunus, Pyrus, Acer, Malus, Sorbur, Caragana arborescens·

Shrubs Camellias, Ribes, Exochorda 'The Bride', Azaleas,* Rhododendron,* Cistus

Border Tulips, Forget-me-nots, Scillas, Lilies of the valley, Helleborus corsicus, Allium, Bluebell, Solomon's Seal, Dicentras

Conservatory Pelargoniums, Fuchsia, Stephanotis floribunda

Climbers Clematis 'Nelly Moser', Clematis montana, Lonicera 'Belgica'

JUNE

Trees Laburnum, Eucalyptus, Robinia 'Frisia', Gleditsia, Pyrus salicifolia

Shrubs Potentilla, Philadelphus, Hebe pinguifolia 'Pagei', Roses, Rubus tridel, Buddleias, Cytisus battandieri, Lavatera

Border Poppies, Allium, Peony, Astrantia, Alchemilla mollis, Helianthemum, Geranium, Hollyhock, Nepeta, Dianthus, Oenothera, Iris, Hemerocallis, Alysum, Campanula

Conservatory Pelargonium, Fuchsia, Plumbago capensis, Lilium

Climbers Eccremocarpus, Lonicera (Honeysuckle), Cobea scandens, Clematis, Hydrangea peteolaris, Passiflora caerulea, Roses, Wisteria

JULY

Trees Eucalyptus

Shrubs Cytisus battandieri, Roses, Buddleia, Potentillas, Abelia, Ceanothus, Ceratostigma willmottianum, Lavendulas

Border Hollyhock, Phormium, Roses, Agapanthus, Ruta graveolens, Scabious, Hostas

Conservatory Streptocarpus, Lilium, Pelargonium, Passiflora, Abutilon

Climbers Actidinia kolomikta, Solanum crispum, Tropaeolum, Jasmines, Honeysuckles, Lathyrus latifolius

AUGUST

Shrubs Lavendula, Fuchsias, Roses

Border Nasturtium, Hemerocallis, Oenothera, Fuchsia, Sedum, Feverfue, Phlox, Penstemon

Conservatory Lilium, Streptocarpus, St. Paulia, Plumbago capensis

Climbers Lonicera halliana, Clematis tangutica, Actidinia kolomikta

SEPTEMBER

Trees Sorbus, Ginko biloba

Shrubs Hydrangeas, Fuchsias, Ceanothus, Ceratostigma willmottianum

Border Sedum, Phormium, Anemone hybrida, Eryngium, Asters, Schizostylis, Scabious

Conservatory Fuchsia corymbiflora, Pelargonium

Climbers Clematis, Lonicera, Passiflora caerulea

OCTOBER

Trees Liquidamber*, Malus 'Golden Hornet', Euonymus 'Red Cascade', Sorbus, Panotia persica

Shrubs Rhus, Cotoneaster, Symphoricarpus

Border Cyclamen neapolitanum, Fuchsia versicolor, Nerine bowdenii, Aster

Conservatory Fuchsia fulgens

Climbers Clematis orientalis

NOVEMBER

Trees Prunus subhirtella 'Autumnalis'

Shrubs Cotoneaster, Berberis, Viburnum farreri

Borders Nerines, Ruta graveolens

Conservatory Cyclamen, Jasminum

Climbers Clematis balearica

DECEMBER

Trees Silver Birch, Prunus subhirtella 'Autumnalis'

Shrubs Viburnum bodnantense, Erica carnea*

Borders Polyanthus, Violets

Conservatory Christmas Cacti, Cyclamen, Jasminum polyanthum, Hippeastrum

Climbers Jasminum nudiflorum, Clematis balearica

Clematis macropetala 'Markhamii', Pulmonaria (soldiers and sailors)

Index